READ THE SIGNS

Radoslav Blagoev

Levels Up
Sofia, 2021

TABLE OF CONTENTS

ACKNOWLEDGMENTS

Of course, *Read the Signs* was inspired by and based upon actual businesses – the thousands of issues in the real life of salespeople and their customers.

This book came to be with the valuable help and support of lots of people; first of all, my loving family, the source of all my motivation and the undying spark of my enthusiasm. Nadya Nenkova, my wonderful editor, with her unparalleled professionalism, energy and optimism, played a key role in the conception of *Read the Signs*. Victoria Grigorova's great design ideas and skill, as well as Gerry Atanasova's illustrations, brought the book to life and made it a finished product.

My thanks to everyone involved in crafting *Read the Signs*; we'll work together again!

INTRODUCTION

"There's no second place in direct sales. You either win, closing the deal, or lose; and the joy of victory is short-lived, because come tomorrow, you'll have to win again."

–Radoslav Blagoev

I wrote this book for those who aspire to become top-notch salespeople. For those managers who would like to motivate their teams with ease and grow their companies. For those who aim at influencing people, indoctrinating them, and convincingly steering the conversation without being aggressive or imposing their opinion at all costs. For people willing to let go of their ego and learn from others' experience. For those who would like to master the skill of *reading the signs.*

The main part of this book is devoted to persuasive skills and effective strategic sales. Many sellers and advertisers owe their failure to the fact that they try to sell people something they do not want, and to the lack of real sales skills. Few realize customers rarely buy what sellers have come to offer them.

This book can help with both direct and distance sales. After reading it, you'll be more persuasive not only while having a conversation or conducting negotiations, but also in your advertisement messages, because the difference between direct sales and marketing is one of scale only.

In recent years, I've come to know different businesses: restaurants, stores, travel agencies, insurance companies, real estate agencies, dental and dermatology clinics, beauty salons, distribution companies, cosmetics companies, software companies, banks, advertisement agencies, furniture manufacturers, recruitment agencies, window manufacturers, etc., which provided me with a broad picture of common business problems. It also inspired me to write this book. **Because the greatest issue of any given business is communication, be it internal or with current and potential customers.**

In this book, I draw upon my twenty years of experience in sales and marketing. I'll share with you the essentials, surmised from my own practice and some of my research and observations. It's up to you whether you'll invest a few hours of your spare time to read it and improve your grasp of persuasive communication. I've honed the skills of thousands of people who trusted me and attended my lectures and seminars. The question is, will you trust me, too?

I believe the book will pay you back handsomely in the coming years, helping you close your deals with ease and making you an expert in persuasive communication, which is a prerequisite for effective marketing. I believe your business will be even greater a success after reading it.

If you'd like to broaden your business knowledge outside the scope of sales, you could spare some more time and read another of my books, ***Business above the Red Line***. It will provide you with various insights about proper business structuring, price formation, market positioning and business development strategies, as well as with numerous examples of my own successes and failures, complemented by ones from my practice as business consultant and sales coach. I'll also share how a piece of seemingly useless information helped me earn 10,000 leva in a single day, at a time when the average monthly salary in Bulgaria was no more than 400 leva, and a few other fascinating stories.

To advertise and sell is an art!

Happy reading.

SELLING IS A **CALLING**

For whatever reason, you've picked *Read the Signs* and decided to invest some of your time to get to know my point of view and perspective on successful sales and exerting influence, and on the power of persuasive communication and strategic marketing. You have your expectations and I sincerely hope I'll be able to meet them.

Not to fail your customers and their expectations is a key principle. More often than not, certain people on the team take care of attracting clients' attention, but then their teammates fail to fulfill those clients' expectations, and the end result is the opposite of the desired one: disappointment.

There is no point in assuring consumers of your high-quality products and claiming to be the best if you are not, or that they'll receive exemplary service if you are not capable of providing it.

Your promises create expectations that have to be met. You must either match consumers' expectations or exceed them. There is nothing worse than wasting money and effort on impressing someone from a distance, only to disappoint them when they actually interact with your business.

I've been involved in sales and marketing for as long as I can remember. I love my job, it fills me with energy and brings me enormous satisfaction. Of course, it has its hard and extremely busy moments, but perhaps without them, one couldn't improve in any sphere, being constantly in one's comfort zone. No significant progress can be made this way. There must be factors that disrupt our comfort. There must be competition that keeps us planning how to retain our market share and develop, otherwise we'll grow lazy, our creativity will languish, and we will not improve in the way we do when our comfort is being disturbed.

In recent years, I've held numerous corporate and open training sessions on various topics related to effective sales and persuasive communication, both online and offline. I've trained many salespeople who chose individual or group sessions either on their own or at the insistence of managers at the companies they worked for.

I've realized more than once, both from personal experience and the rapid improvement of my trainees, how important it is to read the signs in a conversation. This priceless skill gives you an immediate communicative advantage, which grows even greater if you manage to identify the "color" of your opponent.

Being a salesperson is a calling, not a job someone can do half-heartedly, and be successful at it.

Some of the sales reps I worked with believed they were the best, claimed they were able to sell a fridge to an Eskimo, but as you can guess, it was all empty swagger and delusions.

Don't allow your pride and ego to blind you.

Few people are familiar with and capable of using the power of communication. Once you master it, you'll be able to make others believe in your point of view, but of course, it takes lots of practice and effort.

Communication is a power we are not born with.

Some say you are born a salesperson, and there is no other way to become such a skilled manipulator. I agree with that as much as I would agree with a claim that you are born a surgeon, an artist or a writer.

Everyone has their own talent, but without honing it, they cannot hope for success. There's no way a person fond of medicine can become a skilled surgeon without studying and, first and foremost, practicing. They could be born for that, showing a strong disposition for this profession, but knowledge and expertise must be acquired, same as with successful and swaying communication.

Ah, did I mention manipulation? Many people resent the word, claiming they don't wish to be manipulators and exploit others; they'd simply like to sell well, communicate successfully and influence others with ease. They do not want to be manipulators, but they take interest in sales psychology and persuasive communication, in public relations and presentation skills. They are after notable results in marketing and all related spheres.

Come on, let's get real: all this is a form of manipulation, and we are being manipulated every day and in every manner possible. There are so many communication channels, and all are used to influence us one way or another. You shouldn't use manipulation to harm people, but it is by no means a bad thing in itself. Manipulation will allow you to motivate your employees, to exert positive influence on others. It will help you gain an advantage and lend value to your products and services, but don't forget that you shouldn't make promises you are unable to fulfil. You must not give empty hopes if you cannot match consumer expectations. Still, as the word manipulation is often frowned upon, I'll avoid it in later chapters, speaking about **exerting influence** instead.

Don't delude yourself that you can influence others if you are not able to control your own self in the first place. Above all, you should be an expert in influencing yourself: self-motivating and regulating your spontaneity and emotionality. You should control the conversation, learn to listen, not get annoyed at interruptions, and not try to get the upper hand in the exchange by raising your voice. Such behavior does not become a professional. Each outburst and sign of aggression, each time you raise your voice, reduces your chances for a successful deal and definitely does *not* make you the one in control of the conversation.

Perhaps you'd want to argue that some people are impossible to talk to, always interrupting, acting aggressively and provoking you to respond in kind. But I assure you, once you harness the power of persuasive communication, this will no longer be an issue.

Consumers and their behavior are constantly under scrutiny by businesses wishing to guarantee highly effective marketing strategies, increases in sales, market share growth and superiority over the competition.

All professionals strive to build networks of loyal customers, hoping many of those customers will turn into **brand advocates**[1].

But there is one factor that often drastically reduces the efficiency of business and marketing strategies, and that's the staff in direct contact with the end consumer.

I keep hearing talk of the B2B (Business to Business) and B2C (Business to Client) models, but all experienced and successful managers have realized that the most effective business model is H2H (Human to Human).

Let's take a look at the popular **B2B (Business to Business)** model. Have you wondered why it's such a common occurrence for employees to leave a company and start a competing business, taking with them part of their previous employer's clients?

---

[1] A **brand advocate** is a person willing to defend a certain brand from criticism and recommend it, believing wholeheartedly that it is the best option available. They also do not allow others to disparage the brand in question, stand up for it in verbal battles, etc., and do it all voluntarily, without expecting any reward or praise.

Bluntly speaking, if those stolen clients were loyal to the brand, they wouldn't go with the employee and become clients of their new company. But in the years working together, the two parties have forged a good/stable relationship, which is a prerequisite for the clients sticking to the ex-employee in their new enterprise, as a direct competitor of the previous company who failed to win over the employee's loyalty to both itself and the brand.

If a manager was capable of influencing the employee and making them loyal to both their superiors and the brand, the above would never have happened. But this is within the competences of only those managers who recognize the power of communication and know how to yield it not only to sell and attract new customers, but also to retain and motivate their employees.

Let's also have a look at the **B2C (Business to Client)** model. Have you ever stopped being a client of a certain business because a staff member insulted you, the service was unsatisfactory, or you encountered incompetence, insolence, etc.? It happens quite often, and it's a clear indication that however loyal to a certain business the client may be, they still may be lost due to failed communication with the staff.

Nowadays, even in giant hypermarkets where a huge number of buyers come and go every day, the staff is instructed to make customers feel special and provide personal treatment based on the H2H model. Perhaps you've often heard: "Was everything alright with your shopping, Mr. Ivanov?", "Thank you for shopping with us, Mrs. Petrova", "Was everything to your satisfaction?", etc.

That is an attempt to follow this model, albeit not very successfully.

H2H (Human to Human) is a model where each employee considers themselves a key component in the complex business mechanism, and understands their own extreme significance for the creation of a strong brand, which in turn lends value to the offered goods and services. This model leads to a great increase in relationship potential and wins over great numbers of loyal customers. Effective sales do not equal one-time deals. We should put things into perspective and try to encourage a long-term relationship with each and every customer. We should earn their trust and make them appreciate our brand and what we do. That's why I say we should focus on relationship potential.

To do so, it is of utmost importance to master the power of communication. It can be of use in every aspect, from direct sales and business negotiations to the formation and motivation of teams.

Just as merchandising isn't just design and store arrangement, but an entire art, persuasive communication isn't just good manners, a varied vocabulary and proper enunciation. Communication must be studied; it's an amalgam of knowing different personality types, appearance, manners and etiquette, breathing, tone of voice, gestures, creativity, wit, etc.

Of course, without the ability to read the signs, persuasive communication and the value exchange we call a sale will never be entirely successful.

From my work with various salespeople, I've found out that the most valuable of them happen to be real chatterboxes. Their mouths work around the clock, they have an opinion on every topic and often impress it not only on their colleagues, but on their customers as well. They are constantly trying to convince everybody in the truthfulness of their claims and the high quality of the products and/or services they offer. They possess massive amounts of energy, which often places them in leadership positions, and their results are usually higher than average. The term "active listener" is a terra incognita to them. They have never believed that selling is 60% listening and 40% talking. They don't know how to ask questions; they just keep talking and believe that's more than enough for a convincing sale.

It gets even worse over the years, when these people are promoted and start training others, trying to make them their copies. Now you are probably wondering why that would be bad, since those people are good sellers and more successful than most, and it's totally understandable.

Everybody wishes for energetic and assertive people on their team, but unfortunately, those are not real salespeople. If the individuals in question had the opportunity to work along professional dealers, they would realize what a poor job they were doing.

The reason they usually stand out is that most sales teams consist predominantly of ineffective sellers. Companies abound in incompetent and untrained individuals who make lots of calls, hold lots of meetings and consultations, and close very few deals. They explain it with poor marketing environment and the influx of competitors with lower prices, a ready-made excuse for every failure. And they demand better prices and more competitive offers from their superiors, which is an additional strain on business, because I know of no strong brands created through huge discounts and low prices.

When the majority of people on a team are mere consultants, some of them additionally crippled by their huge egos, the energetic talkers I mentioned get ahead, because they at least achieve good results.

Their most common problem is, they fail to form relationships with their clients, pursuing instead a greater number of deals per day, which later turn out to be one-time deals. They rarely hear the client's actual needs or see opportunities for expanding on sales, and that's why I'm saying they are not the perfect salespeople. Nobody can deny their results, but if they could channel their energy properly and learn to read the signs in the conversation, which is closely related to listening, they would be even more successful. If they could exploit the potential of their relationship with the client, they would sell many times more.

There are lots of companies where the cost of attracting a new customer greatly exceeds the profit from the first sale made to said customer. In such cases, real profit is earned only after a second, or even a third sale. This makes it necessary for salespeople to develop long-term relationships and monitor their future potential.

Of course, it is all relative, since some business models do not allow for repeated sales, so no long-term relationship is needed there. But when seeking loyal clients and partnerships, special skills are of primary importance; and who would turn down more deals, even if they were one-time?

Truth is, the number of professional salespeople and skilled manipulators who have remained in others' employ, is quite small. I shouldn't speak in numbers because they won't be based on official statistics, but in my estimation, they should be no more than 5 to 10%.

The reason is that these people are aware of their abilities, and they can rarely negotiate a remuneration with no upper limit that depends entirely on results achieved, although most companies hiring sales reps claim to offer one.

At first, everybody starts with a basic salary and stimulating bonuses, but the moment a sales rep begins accumulating a pay too high for their managers' liking, new bonus schemes are introduced, the targets are raised dramatically, the commission rate is lowered, and the sales rep realizes there is indeed a limit, and not a very high one at that.

Managers believe the sales rep won't quit because they have invested significant effort in order to achieve such enviable results, and besides, the salary, though limited, is still "a winner". On the other hand, if the sales rep leaves the company, their clients will be inherited by a new one, who will receive an even smaller pay as they get everything on a silver platter. They'll earn a high commission rate only for new customers they have found on their own. Thus, the company profits even more.

Of course, although sometimes applied, this is a decidedly ineffective model, because people are a company's greatest asset, and losing a successful rep only to gain a bit more at their expense is a ludicrous scheme that can only lead to serious losses for both the company and its owner.

There are several risks when limiting a sales rep's income. Feeling offended, said rep can quit and start working for a competing company, taking some of their old loyal customers with them. They may also launch their own company, which will again involve attracting known customers from their previous employ. But even if none of this happens, the new rep inheriting the old one's job will not be able to retain all of their clients.

Professionals are able to communicate so easily with different types of customers that they quickly become their favorites, earn their trust and put effort into maintaining it. A new rep will most likely lack these skills, which will lead to acrid disappointment on part of the customers and will inevitably reflect on results.

On the other hand, these poor results will be noticed by the managers, who will blame the new rep, and so, little by little, a thing that took years of hard work to build will be ruined in mere months.

Professional salespeople never disclose their know-how; they often share fictional tales with their colleagues, but never reveal their cards. They tell others what the latter want to hear to keep them at peace and out of their hair. They often pretend in front of envious coworkers that they've hit an obstacle or messed up an important deal and won't earn much, which is a balm for the resentful person's soul.

If envy and spite are like food for some, such salespeople can give it to them to avoid being eaten up.

A good sales rep's caseload couldn't be assigned to another without incurring losses, because there always is secret know-how that will disappear along with them. Those reps know that they should always share only what they know, but never all they know.

A sales rep that closes lots of deals can often be viewed as a company inside the company. That's why they should be treated with caution, because both their contributions and the losses they may bring about can be considerable.

To be an energetic and talkative enthusiast is not sufficient, and mere enthusiasm and long experience in this extremely complex and difficult line of work are not reason enough to call yourself an expert salesperson.

I hope the information I share in this book will help you become excellent salespeople and marketing experts, capable of influencing not only separate individuals, but whole audiences. I would call direct sales the art of asking questions, listening carefully, reading the signs and making use of them at the right time.

A sale is the solution to a problem that cannot be identified if the seller keeps talking instead of listening. When this sort of thing happens, you solve a problem of your own making. You provide a solution which you yourself consider an opportunity, but the client can view it as a disadvantage.

Now's the time to differentiate between a good dealer and a good consultant, because these are two entirely separate occupations. Most of those who call themselves dealers are in fact consultants. They do not create consumer needs and rarely attempt to solve problems. More often than not, they introduce the client to a product and its qualities, or a service and its advantages, but fail to see that for some, these will be good and add value, while for others they may be a problem.

Now comes the story of the salesman strategist, and immediately after, a few other stories about strategic sales that I believe you could easily modify to fit your business and marketing strategy.

THE SALESMAN **STRATEGIST**

For the last week, Peppy[2] had been working for a company specializing in the import and distribution of fast-moving consumer goods. He was the newest employee and was currently in training to get a feel for the business. Selling was a real passion for him and he had the gift of

---

[2] In Bulgaria, the name Peppy is a shortened version of Petko or Peter, or their female equivalents. – translator's note

winning people's hearts. In a month, Peppy knew the names of all the other employees. He was very outgoing, funny and charismatic. He easily befriended everyone, with the exception of the envious types.

> *"Envy keeps no holidays."*
>
> –Francis Bacon

The company was not very large – it employed about forty people, half of them sales reps. Peppy started in a new area, and at first orders were scarce. That didn't worry him though – for him, selling was fun, and it came naturally. It ran in his veins, as they say. He struck up relationships, talked to people who could start ordering from him. Told jokes and made them laugh. He was never in a hurry, always stopping for a coffee and a pleasant chat. The rest of the sales reps mocked him and didn't see him as a threat, thinking him funny and useless. They had work to do, and no time to waste on coffees and idle chats with clients. The more orders they collected, the more they would earn, since their pay was formed by a low basic salary, complemented by high commission rates.

Here came payday, and Peppy received a rather humble check. He hadn't met even half the monthly target, but that was not a problem because he had the first three months to develop his area, and he could do it at his own pace.

Since his arrival at the company, the atmosphere grew friendlier. In the mornings, when all gathered in the office before starting their daily tours to visit clients, you could often hear laughter. Peppy told funny stories or waved around a client order worth no more than his morning treat at the nearby cafeteria. He also paid compliments to the ladies, who blossomed under his attention like flowers in spring.

The young rep's area was becoming more profitable, the orders grew in number, and he remained just as laid-back and ready to smile. Some found it odd, others hadn't liked him since the beginning. They envied his pleasant appearance and easy-going personality, and were annoyed when their colleagues considered him special. But Peppy really was special, he had a gift. He was able to organize and motivate people, could make them laugh or think. And unlike most of his coworkers, he was unpredictable. No wonder he had so many friends both at work and outside it.

One morning, Peppy said to all sales reps, "Hey you, weaklings, what do you say we hold a competition today? Whoever brings in most orders, wins a crate of beer."

"Peppy, you're one of the worst reps here – why offer a competition when you have zero chances of winning?" said Ivan. He was a leading rep in the company and not one of Peppy's fans.

"*You* could win though, Vanka. I'm in it for the challenge and the fun. Let's have fun while working, and let the best man win. What do you say, are you in?"

"Sure, Peppy. If you want, I can even place another bet with you alone: I'll collect twice as many orders as you today."

"Okay, if that'll make you happy, let's do it."

Peppy didn't do anything out of the ordinary that day, just kept steadily working his area, convinced in his future success. He knew it was only a question of time for the orders to skyrocket. The pay was important to him because he saved up to launch his own business.

At the end of the day, all reps returned to the office to register the day's orders. Peppy had already bought a crate of beer and waited for the others to come in. They all cheered, and even Ivan shook his head with a smile and grabbed a beer from the crate.

All sales reps registered high numbers of orders, which didn't escape the notice of their manager. Tony left his office and started questioning his reps, looking for the reason for these excellent results. Imagine his surprise when he found out they'd been competing for a crate of beer, compliments of the new guy. He patted Peppy on the shoulder, asking him why he had done it.

Peppy said with a smile, "Tony, when I play poker, I never reveal my cards. Now I have to either lie to you or say nothing at all."

"Lie then, Peppy, I don't appreciate people ignoring my questions."

"I try to keep people in top shape, Tony."

Tony laughed at the quick and witty reply. He was pleased with the day's work, but he himself was not good at motivating his people. He knew the rates he offered weren't enough to make their blood boil. Tony was stern but fair: he had developed a bonus scheme and everybody knew what pay to expect at any given time, but beside that, he didn't know what to do. He had tried introducing games a few times, taking his employees on team building activities to draw them closer, but it did nothing to keep his team on their toes. The sales reps often didn't make good use of their working hours; some attended to private matters while on the clock, while others didn't enjoy their job and were near useless. But these details were lost on Tony; he only watched the amount of orders and tried to keep the company out of the red.

Unlike him, Peppy had a clear goal, and he was motivated, passionate, energetic and consistent. He understood people and trusted his gut. And so, not long after, there came the day when Peppy ended the month with the highest number of orders processed. He never talked about work and the other reps didn't keep an eye on his daily doings. His coworkers had pegged him as a great talker who didn't do much work; their judgment was completely off.

All were amazed by his results, some thinking it blind luck, but the figures didn't lie.

Tony praised the young rep and whisked him aside for a private talk. "Buddy, you've done wonders. I don't know how you pulled this off, but well done."

"Thanks, Tony. I'm just doing my job."

"Yes, you are, and you're mighty good at it. The atmosphere changed a lot since you came here. You've been lifting people's spirits, and that's great. I'm wondering, if you propose a competition now, will they agree to it?"

"Ha-ha, no, I wouldn't propose one now."

"Why not?"

"I have my reasons, Tony, I told you – I never reveal my cards."

"But I'm your boss, and if I tell you to propose a competition, you have to do it."

"No, Tony, you're wrong. You can't force me to hold a competition. We have a contract; you pay me to sell. I do my best to bring in good profit. I like my job and, as you can see, I get better results every day. This exhausts our relationship."

"Wise words, Peppy, but I'm still your boss."

"That's right, Tony, but I prefer the word "employer". But if you think there's conflict between us, and you don't appreciate the way I do my job, we can always put an end to our working relations."

"Aren't you afraid that in such a case, all your effort would have been in vain?"

"Tony, do you really think it would be?"

Tony realized the boy was tough. It was the first time he heard him speak seriously, not joking in the slightest. Peppy knew no fear. He believed in himself and didn't let anyone infringe on his freedom. He had steady relationships with most clients and knew they worked with him, not the company. And Tony was aware of that. He was an old timer and had no intention of firing his future CEO. "I like you, kid. No one has dared talk to me like that before. But you are right. I won't interfere with your work. Go show those lazy dogs how one becomes a CEO."

Mulling over these last words, Peppy left Tony's office.

"Hey, Peppy, how did it go – did the boss reward you with candy?" said Ivan, trying to hurt Peppy, but his joke fell flat.

Peppy parried the nasty remark with a smile and a nod, and left the room.

Next month, Ivan and a couple of other reps, borderline workaholics, vowed to get their top positions back. But they had no time to visit extra clients, while Peppy had worked around this problem. He went to his clients only for coffee. He had instructed them to make their orders via phone. Thus he had enough time to visit a few clients every day, giving them his full attention. Most of them didn't consider Peppy an especially successful sales rep, but they weren't bothered by it and genuinely enjoyed his company. He was good at making others laugh and entertaining them, knew how to listen, and people relished talking to him, even seeking advice and moral support. Some openly relied on Peppy's words to raise their self-esteem and motivate them to pursue success. They considered him a valued companion, even a friend. This was the very reason they trusted him more and agreed to order via phone; his tactics worked like a charm. Clients often told him they'll place their order only if he came in person, because they missed his company, but nobody was capable of refusing him flat out. Peppy knew people well, and that made him such a successful sales rep.

The month was over and he was again on top: most business done and highest number of orders processed. It was unbelievable, and everybody wondered how he managed it. Most sales reps admired him00, but a few, Ivan among them, considered his success a personal failure. Peppy stole their fame, stole their income, and made them feel like losers. This had to change. Ivan and a couple of other reps started concocting a plan to upstage Peppy.

But Peppy was ready for them. He expected as much; people like them were old news to him, so transparent and shallow. They were always straightforward and easy to predict, and he knew how to counter their attacks. He had gathered a crew, winning over all important people in the office who spurned malice and envy. Peppy had them on his side, but asked them to pretend they didn't like him.

And so, Ivan started to execute his well-thought out plan to remove Peppy and reclaim his position as the company's top seller. He convinced the storeroom guy to hide some goods and report them stolen, at the same time asking the accountant to conceal an order so they can blame Peppy for failing to hand it in, stealing the client's money instead. Ivan had put up a client to calling and claiming he had placed the missing order and paid it to Peppy. Ivan also instructed the parking clerk to say he had noticed a huge overdraw of fuel for Peppy's company car, which most likely meant Peppy was stealing fuel. Ivan believed that after all this came to light, Peppy would be fired. Tony detested theft and wouldn't ignore a person stealing, no matter how much profit he brought the company.

Use your brain!

The very next day, Peppy already knew about all of Ivan's arrangements and schemes, and the colleagues decided it would be best to turn Ivan's infernal ploy against him. The accountant gave Peppy the order she was supposed to hide, the storeroom attendant gave him the goods he was supposed to steal, and Stoil, who was in charge of the company's car park, gave him the spare keys from Ivan's vehicle. Peppy bore a small hole in the tank of his own company car, and went home.

The next day, Peppy came to the office early. He put the missing order in the glove compartment of Ivan's company car and the reportedly stolen goods in his trunk, using the spare keys Stoil had given him. He also tore through one of the tires with a nail he left in the tire. Then he made himself coffee and waited.

Everybody arrived and Ivan signaled his client to call and complain about his goods not being delivered. At the same time, the storeroom attendant announced some merchandise have been stolen, and Stoil told Tony about the missing fuel. On the surface, everything went according to Ivan's plan. Now he was eager for Tony to blame Peppy for it all and fire him.

And indeed, soon Tony emerged from his office, angry, and called Peppy in for a talk. "What's going on here, kid, have you started stealing from me?"

"I appreciate your trust, Tony."

"Don't play the fool, I'm serious."

"Tony, to what do I owe these suspicions and accusations?"

"Stoil told me your car had been burning through the fuel."

"I'm sorry, Tony, I noticed the sharp stench of diesel only this morning, and then I saw the tank was pierced and leaked fuel."

"A client called and said he paid you last week, but no order had been logged with the accountant."

"Really? Which client?"

"Let me see, yes, here it is. One Mr. Kirilov."

"Tony, I know all my clients by name and he's not one of them, he's never ordered anything from me. But judging by the address, it must be one of Ivan's. That's within his perimeter."

"The storeroom boy said some goods went missing."

"That's really bad, Tony, perhaps you should install cameras."

"Hmm, come and show me where your tank leaks from."

"Sure, let's go."

The two left the office where Ivan wore a sly smile. They reached the car and Tony inspected the damage. "Thank god the car didn't catch fire. Tell Stoil to have it repaired and give you another for the time being. But the other issues still stand, and I won't leave them be." Tony turned to go back to the building, but saw Ivan's flat tire. "Ivan, didn't you see your tire's punctured? Ask someone to help you change it and go. It's getting late, when are you going to collect today's orders?"

A few people hurried to help Ivan replace the tire more quickly. He opened the trunk to take out the spare, and there stood the merchandise missing from the storeroom. Joro, a colleague of Ivan's, asked him about it, but Ivan only kept shaking his head, baffled. Someone called Tony down, and a moment later, Ivan spluttered he had no idea where these goods came from. "Perhaps it had been ordered and I was to deliver it, but I've forgotten. I don't know, there's some misunderstanding", Ivan kept explaining.

Tony asked him to check his receipts and see if someone had indeed ordered the goods. Ivan was an old employee and Tony trusted him. The sales rep opened the glove compartment and handed Tony the folder of receipts. Unfortunately, it also held the missing one, which Tony had suspected Peppy of stealing only moment ago. "How would you explain this receipt from last week?"

"To be honest, I can't, Tony, I must have forgotten to hand it to the accountant."

"But the goods are paid for. A client called today to complain he didn't get them. You claimed Peppy took the order and I doubted him. I thought he was stealing from me, and now I find the receipt with you. Care to explain?"

"I'm sorry, Tony, there must be some mix-up."

Then the truth dawned on Tony. He realized it was an attempt at sabotage, shook his head and smiled. "You screwed up, Vanka, screwed up big time. I won't be made to look like a fool! Don't bother coming in tomorrow. You're fired!"

Then, to everyone's surprise, Peppy intervened. "Tony, let's not go too far. Ivan's a good rep, without him the team will have difficulty meeting the monthly target. You know he wouldn't steal from you. He just tried to set me up because he hates me. But after what happened today, I think there will be no more trouble."

"Kid, I don't know how you tricked Ivan into falling in his own trap, but this month both of you will receive no bonuses."

Tony left for his office, still angry, but Peppy called after him, "Hey, Tony, are you up for a competition? If someone manages to collect more orders than me or Ivan this month, let our bonuses be spread among the other reps; if not, they go to you."

"I like that, Peppy, let's have a competition with your bonuses as the reward." Tony's spirits lifted and he went back to his office. He was lucky he didn't need to kick anyone out – both Ivan and Peppy were valuable. And now the competition was likely to make this month more profitable than ever.

Ivan left the others to replace his tire and went after Peppy. "Hey, champion!"

"Oh, to what do I owe this honor?"

"Look, Peppy, I wanted you to know I don't hate you. I'm ashamed of what I did, and I'm sorry. I don't expect you to say yes, but I'd like to buy you a drink after work."

"Sure, let's do it." Peppy didn't want any enemies. And he was well aware that turning your enemy into a friend was a winning strategy.

At the end of the day, Ivan processed his orders and he and Peppy went for a beer. Ivan really felt guilty, and awfully embarrassed. He had always been a top rep, and today all his colleagues thought he was a schemer. "Peppy, you have always been so decent, and I don't know what got into me. Falling on deceit to try and keep my position."

"Ivan, you'd just do anything to retain your top status. You are a sore loser, aren't you?"

"I can't stomach failure. Aren't *you* willing to do anything to win?"

"Me? No, it's not about being the best in the company. I'm trying to earn as much as possible because I'm saving for my own business."

"Wow, having your own company. Sounds awesome. Have you decided what it would be?"

"Sure, but I don't want to talk about it now. This month, thanks to you, I'll hardly earn more than pocket money. Why did you have to act so stupid?"

"I know, you're right. I'll try to pay you back sometime."

"Vanka, do you know why I offered Tony to let the others compete with us this month?"

"No, why? I was just about to ask you."

"Well, I plan on bringing in fewer orders this month. Let's give our bonuses to the team. Better they have them than Tony."

"Ha-ha, the old man will see red when he realizes how you played him."

"Yes, I know Tony won't like it. But I'm not better off either, what with that beggar's salary."

"So you're not sucking up to Tony, you're even ready to challenge him?"

"Oh, I've never sucked up to anybody. It's all tactics. I believe in my abilities, and I told you, I don't plan on being here more than a couple of years. Then I'll launch my own business."

"Peppy, you're a great guy. I was wrong about you, blinded by my own pride. Please forgive me. And be sure you can count on me. We may even become business partners one day."

"I know, Vanka. You heard what I told Tony today – that we'll hardly make trouble in the future."

"How can you be so sure?"

"Why, am I wrong?"

"No, of course not, *we* won't be trouble anymore. But I think you'll have some at the end of the month, when he realizes you've tricked him."

They both burst out laughing, finished their beers in one go and asked for the check. It was the beginning of a deep friendship. Ivan accepted that Peppy was a better salesperson, and was ready to follow him in his future business venture.

This month, they both worked without straining too much. They spent much of their time together, deep in talk, and often discussed the business Peppy planned on starting. Peppy's ambition was so strong and contagious that Ivan also started looking forward to the day they'd have enough capital to enter the real battle. The project had the blood of both of them boiling, and they started sharing a little about their intentions with those colleagues they were closest to, attracting even more potential partners in their shared venture.

At the end of the month, several sales reps had achieved higher results than Ivan and Peppy. Tony kept looking at the logs and laughing. "What's the matter, guys, you've had a bad month, it seems?"

"Yes, Tony, we didn't get many orders and they beat us."

"Hey, kid, do you really think I believe a word of this rubbish? You tricked me the moment you proposed this competition."

"Noting of the sort, Tony, the guys won fair and square."

"Okay, you outsmarted me. I'll give your bonuses to the other reps. And I'm wondering, should I do the same next month as well?"

"Sure, Tony, it's your decision. But if you plan on doing it, please tell us so that we can take the month off."

Now they were all laughing, and even Tony appreciated Peppy's wit. "Okay then, no more punishment, give it your all next month and let the machine run on full power."

Tony was very pleased with Peppy. Everything changed for the better: people enjoyed themselves and worked with a passion. A few people left the team, but it didn't reflect on the business in any way – the others took their clients and even worked their new areas better. But Tony knew nothing lasted forever. He expected the happy times to be offset by not so successful ones, again the work of the young rep. But there was nothing he could do, so he decided to enjoy success and let the chips fall where they may.

Peppy kept improving his results. Ivan followed his example, and thanks to the new tricks he learned, he also became more successful. Some of their coworkers copied the top reps and grew, too. There's nothing better than a team choosing their captain on their own and following his lead.

Now Tony communicated mainly with Peppy; without appointing him department manager, he had in fact become one.

Nearly two years passed, and Peppy and his future business partners managed to collect their startup capital. Now he had to share the grim news with Tony: to tell him he was leaving. Worse still, he was taking Ivan and three other good reps with him. It would be a hard blow for Tony, but ultimately, the end justified the means. Everyone had the right to pursue their dreams. It was now time for them to end their contracts.

Peppy asked to meet with Tony so that they could have a serious talk. Tony waited in his office, bracing himself for the bad news.

"Tony, I have to tell you something you won't like. But you're the best boss, and I want to be honest with you."

"Cut the act, Peppy, and out with it."

"I have to leave the company."

"Why? Is anything the matter? You earn even more than I do!"

"Yes, I earn decent money, but my mind's made up."

"Can you at least tell me why? I wouldn't like to be losing more reps due to some fault of mine."

"Actually, that's the other piece of bad news. Four more people are quitting along with me, one of them Ivan."

"Yeah, it's getting better and better. You'll be leaving me high and dry."

"Don't worry, we won't go right away but wait for you find replacements, even a couple of months if necessary."

"Okay, that's good. It'll give me some time to come up with a solution. But why are you all resigning, aren't you going to tell me?"

"I am, Tony. I've always wanted to have a business of my own. Now the others and I are starting our own company, and so we must leave you."

"I see. And let me guess, you'll be competition."

"Indeed. I'm sorry, Tony!"

"Don't fret it, kid." Tony chuckled and asked for all those quitting to gather in his office.

He knew this day would come, and was happy that they were leaving to start their own business, not after receiving better offers from the competition. He was an experienced businessman and already had an offer he hoped the guys would accept.

Now they were all in his office, expecting serious criticism and the exchange of harsh words. Tony asked everyone to switch off their phones, doing the same himself. Then he called his assistant and instructed her he was not to be disturbed, even if the building got on fire. Heavens, what was about to happen?

"Guys, I admire you. I'm especially pleased with Peppy and Ivan. Enemies yesterday, and now partners. I consider you all family. I've always done right by each of you. Perhaps I've been a little stern, but I'd like to think, fair. You've decided to strike on your own, and that's great. But being good reps doesn't mean your business will be a success."

"Tony, don't try to talk us out of it, it's decided."

"Please, don't interrupt me, Vanka. Just hear me out and then I'll give you the floor. How much money do you have?"

"About 150,000 leva."

"Okay, that's decent money, perhaps it'll be enough for a start. Do you know how much I've put into my company so far?"

"Perhaps a million?"

"No, Peppy, just the merchandise I have in storage is worth more. I've invested nearly two million. But this business does not require investment in machinery. People are my equipment. I've been developing this company for over ten years now. Ivan's been with me for five of them, and you for two. Everything I've achieved, it's thanks to the people working for me. And here you are, telling me I'll have to part with my best assets. This would mean moving backwards instead of forwards. But I don't have a choice. I don't own you, so I'll have to let you go.

"But first, I have a proposition for you. I would offer you shares in my business in return for your capital, making you shareholders. Turning down such an opportunity would be a mistake. Or, I could become a partner in your new company, investing an amount even greater than yours. What do you say?"

Nobody expected such a turn of events, they were all caught unawares. Even Peppy's sharp mind was overwhelmed. The guys could become investors in Tony's company or start their own with much greater capital. Tony had extensive experience and good reputation in this sphere. But which was the better offer?

"Guys, I see you're confused, go and think over my offers. When you are ready, please tell me what you've decided. In my opinion, you'd be better off as investors in this company. It has already been on the road for a long time, and it takes care of itself. We could implement some changes together; your views are more modern, and your blood is boiling. I know how I felt when I started my business. And in case you're wondering what shares I'm going to give you, here's the deal. You get 19% of the company. 5% each for Peppy and Ivan, and 3% each for the rest of you. You are well aware that's worth much more than 150,000 but I want you to see how much I value you."

That was a great opportunity for the guys. But it was one for Tony as well. He could have young and energetic partners who had plenty of motivation and drive for success. They knew the business inside and out, and were worth ten of his other sales reps. In addition, they wouldn't be his direct competitors, as would be the case if they started their own company.

The boys went for a beer, smiling and still unable to believe their luck. They could own shares in Tony's company.

"Peppy, all that would never have happened if you haven't come to work with us. I would have spent years and years as a regular rep, until Tony eventually kicked me out."

"That's right, guys, we're given a chance. People often let chances pass them by, overwhelmed by their fears. But I'm not such a person and I think I'll accept Tony's offer. What do you say?"

"I'm with you, Peppy."

"Me too!"

They all agreed to it: they'd become shareholders in Tony's company.

In the morning, when they told him their decision, Tony took a stack of papers out of his desk, passing it to them to sign.

"Tony, how did you know we'd accept?"

"Guys, I offered you shares because I believe you're smart and capable. Who'd be crazy enough to turn down such an offer?"

They all laughed and signed the papers. Now they were officially co-owners of the company. Peppy achieved his goal, and all who followed him felt lucky they knew him. And Tony's intuition helped him out yet again. He wasn't very creative, but always trusted his gut.

And here came the first shareholders' general meeting, and they unanimously chose Peppy for marketing director. They all counted on his gift for motivating people. It was a key factor for the success of the sales department.

A **WRONG APPROACH** TO A CLIENT WITH A CONSCIOUS NEED

As a sales coach, I often accompany salespeople on their meetings, and then we analyze and improve their communication skills. While training a team of real estate agents, I encountered a curious situation.

One client wished to buy a house. He had provided the agency with his criteria, and one day, the broker in charge of the search came across a great offer and scheduled a viewing.

While we were at this magnificent house, the agent, Ignat, kept talking, listing its many advantages, while the client only nodded and took in his surroundings in silence.

The agent praised the fireplace, how expensive it was and what powerful firebox it had, able to cover the whole living area, and so on and so forth. When we entered the yard, the agent kept chatting, explaining what a great pool it had, and well-kept too, while the client still nodded, jotting notes in a small, black and a little crumpled notebook. He also made strange faces from time to time, perhaps due to a nervous tic.

When the agent exhausted his list and had nothing more to say about the property, having showered the client with more facts than the owner himself probably knew, he asked, "So, what do you think of this house, Mr. Stoimenov? Is it to your liking?"

"To be honest, guys, I have some issues with it."

"Tell us what's bothering you, Mr. Stoimenov."

"I don't want my house to have a fireplace. I consider them very dangerous and capable of causing a serious fire. As I already told you, my children are young, and I never know what can come into their heads. So I'll have to invest in removing the fireplace and installing a new heating system, because if I understood you correctly, that's the main heating mechanism now.

"Moreover, I don't like the pool and I wonder how much it will cost me to fill it in. I'm not a fan of pools, one of the kids can fall in and drawn, and it requires serious upkeep. On the other hand, I like the house, but some of the things that lend it such a great value are useless to me. And it will need a lot of additional investment. Could it be possible to ask the owner if he's willing to cut down the price by 10,000 euro in view of the repairs I'm planning, namely the dismantling of the fireplace, the filling up of the pool and the installment of a new heating system?"

"Sure, Mr. Stoimenov, I'll have a word with the client, but I doubt it he'll consider such a discount. Besides, the fact you don't like these extras doesn't make them useless, everybody would like a pool in their house, and a grand fireplace like this here. Such accessories are expensive to build, and most people find them really valuable."

"Perhaps you're right, Ignat, but next time we view a property, please take into account my opinions and needs."

"But of course, Mr. Stoimenov, we'll have them in mind for next time."

By this point, Ignat was completely out of his element. His insistence on the value of the accessories was unnecessary, but he didn't know what else to say. Claiming everybody would want a fireplace and a pool, and suggesting it wasn't the client's business to spurn them, was yet another of the agent's mistakes. It implied Mr. Stoimenov had no choice but to like what everybody else liked.

Ignat had spoken about the house at such length, and lent so much value to these accessories the client found useless, that now he had no choice but to offer another house for viewing, or negotiate a reduced price with the owner, which he was highly unlikely to get. The house matched all the client's other criteria such as location, size and price, but the deal fell through.

What was invested in this meeting was lost. I say invested, because each meeting is an investment.

If a salesperson would like to earn 5,000 leva a month, they have to calculate how much each meeting would cost – in this case, each property viewing. They should be aware of each deal's potential and spare enough time for researching their clients' needs in order to achieve better results.

If we allot 180 hours a month to work, and wish to make 5,000 leva, this means we move at 27 leva per hour and 0.46 leva per minute. This meeting cost Ignat at least ten hours. This is the time he invested in doing research and finding a suitable house for viewing, arranging the viewing itself, traveling to the house, doing the viewing and getting back to his office.

If Ignat had more information in advance, the viewing may not have occurred, or he could have spent more time looking for a more suitable offer – which now he'd have to look for again.

If Ignat had given the client an opportunity to speak, if he had asked the right questions and had been able to read the signs manifest in the conversation, the situation may have been different: the accessories stripped of their value and rendered insignificant in the process of price formation.

The mistakes in this case are very easy to spot:

» There is insufficient information about the client's initial criteria, so the client's consumer profile has not been properly compiled;

» Ignat takes it upon himself to lend value to things he finds valuable, not knowing if the same holds true for his client – a common misconception;

» Ignat dominates the conversation, leaving his client to listen, instead of doing the opposite;

» Ignat does not see a single sign he could use in the battle of words, because you can only notice the signs while you listen.

And since I mentioned Ignat lending value to things he himself considers valuable, I'd like to explain here what it means to only follow your own map. Imagine a historical map, a topographic map and a regular road map. Some consider the topographic map really valuable, while for others it would be of no use. Some find historical maps fascinating, while others cannot fathom what their purpose is. Likewise, each of us has their own map, tracking what's important in their life. All significant things are marked there, along with all those of little value. And of course, they are different for every individual. That's why we shouldn't make decisions for others, or impose on them our opinions on what's good and what's valuable.

> *You can only notice the signs while you listen.*
> Radoslav Blagoev

Imagine we could hold this meeting again. We would start by asking some questions.

"Mr. Stoimenov, please take a look around and tell me what you like and what bothers you, and then I'll say a bit more about the house."

If the client were honest, he'd now share his issues with the fireplace and the pool, and he'd also say what was to his liking, giving us the opportunity to add and subtract value.

Let's say, the client told us he didn't like the pool and the fireplace and planned on removing them, but he was impressed by the stone siding and the two large beams on the ceiling.

Now we could point the conversation in a different direction:

"Mr. Stoimenov, it's clear to me that this is the right house for you!"

That would probably confuse the client because it defies all logic. We claim the house was ideal for him despite the existence of things he didn't like, but are costly, and his intention of doing away with them, which is again costly.

"The current owner, Martin, specifically asked if he could take away the firebox, because it holds sentimental value for him. Being quite old, **it is near worthless**, but it was a gift from a dear friend of his. Perhaps, if you don't intend to use the fireplace anyway, it won't be a problem to give it to him?

"Moreover, when buying the house, Martin also didn't want the pool and managed to strip its value from the price of the property, but instead of filling it in, he kept it covered and never used it. That's why, **it is not included in the price of the property now as well**. Of course, you can fill it in if you'd like, or keep it covered like Martin did. I would keep it, but if you prefer, I could offer Martin to pay for having it demolished and grassed over. What do you think?

"I'm glad you noticed the ceiling beams. At first glance, there's nothing extraordinary about them, but they have curious history. Martin mentioned that when he bought the house, the beams caught his attention too, and when he asked the then owners about them, they shared an intriguing tale. The original builders of this house were two brothers. Their forefathers had planted several trees, intending them to be used for their grandchildren's home, and bring the family happiness and wellbeing. To build this house, the brothers fell two of these trees and used them for the ceiling beams, just as intended. Later, the brothers married abroad, settled there and sold the property to Martin. He in turn is a successful businessmen, and with things going really well for him in recent years, he's now moving to England with his entire family.

"But enough talk. You must be getting bored, I strayed too far from the subject. Tell me, what do you think, Mr. Stoimenov?"

To drive the point home, many people would say outright "Mr. Stoimenov, it seems this house brings good luck", but this is not the right approach. We don't need to spell these things out, they are well illustrated by the story. If we highlight them even more, it may raise suspicion about their truthfulness. Leave the key points in shadow, let them be implied by context. It's not necessary to bring them to the foreground; it's not what successful and subtle communication is about.

You saw how we could undermine the useless things and lend value to those appreciated. Presented in such light, the accessories Mr. Stoimenov does not like are belittled and disparaged, while the beams' worth is accentuated.

People like Mr. Stoimenov have predominantly Green or Yellow personalities. You'll learn more about the different colors later in the book. Don't bother looking for that section now; I'll use colors in the examples I provide, and when the time comes to read about them, you'll quickly find answers to the questions you have now, and you'll remember it all much easier.

In the example above, there's not enough information to determine the color, but a person taking notes in silence is definitely not Blue or Red, which means one of the other two colors is predominant in his personality.

Greens really appreciate a competent consultant, well versed in all the particulars; they are interested in technical details, so the origin story will demonstrate competence, as well as in-depth knowledge of the property's history. It's possible they pepper you with questions, but that's nothing to worry about, because questions are a show of interest, and interest is the prerequisite for a deal.

Each awkward question can get an excellent answer as long as a person has a sharp and well-trained mind, and has mastered the art of communication.

If the dominant color is yellow, that means this person puts safety first, but also pays attention to all energy sources and the story of previous inhabitants. Yellows wouldn't allow their family to live in a place expounding bad energy or obvious risks. Constantly caring about others is their calling.

Getting an analytical mind confused is a great strategy, it makes the person lose focus and gives you an advantage in the conversation. When we tell Mr. Stoimenov we are now sure it's the right house for him, we baffle him and make him follow our argument closely, then impress upon him how little value the useless things have, while promoting the ones he appreciates.

The conversation has now taken a different turn, and the pool and fireplace are no longer a valid reason for demanding a discount.

Of course, it's all too easy to guess how things may have gone; this is just an analysis of an ineffective meeting, and the imaginary talk only serves to point you in the right direction.

A conversation can go a dozen, or even a hundred different ways, but wherever it leads, it's vital to ask the right questions and listen carefully to the answers, so that we can notice the signs and use them.

We have no way of adding or stripping value if we don't know what matters for the other and what not.

In the above case, we have a client with a conscious need, but that does not mean we cannot reshape his requirements so that the thing we offer became an object of desire for our customer.

I suppose this example made it perfectly clear why I emphasize the difference between a consultant and a true salesperson.

Consultants often judge people and decide for them. They rush into conclusions about who is going to buy something and who isn't; who has money, who is just window-shopping and who is an actual client. They don't create needs, but just follow a routine.

Things get even more complex in direct sales, since there you need to create a need. That's what sets the best salespeople apart. To create a need, to provoke interest and steer someone into buying something they didn't feel the need for until this very moment, is completely different from just providing for someone who came to you with a conscious need in mind.

The following story illustrates how you create a need and give your client the opportunity to make a purchase.

DIRECT SALES OF A TRENDY AND WELL-KNOWN PRODUCT TO A PERSON WITH AN UNCONSCIOUS NEED

The struggle to stay fit has generated lots of niche markets and continues to spawn more. Fitness instructors, dieticians, specialized video courses, seminars, webinars, guidance websites, food supplements, fitness retreats, cosmetic procedures and what not. A great number of activities which find their audience in out-of-shape people who have decided to get fit and/or improve their health.

Now's the time to mention that, according to statistics, it's extremely expensive to advertise and sell prevention products, because people are proven to spend whatever needed to cure themselves, but next to nothing to protect their health. Many don't invest much in oral hygiene, some even forego brushing their teeth, but when their smile starts failing tooth by tooth, they are ready to spend a fortune to make it shining and impressive once again. The reason is, people tend to see the world to their advantage – but you'll read more about this inclination, and how to capitalize on it in conversation, later on in the book. Now let me get back to the story of selling vibrating belts, which is an illustration of selling a well-known product to a person with an unconscious need.

In 2001, the cost of these belts in Bulgaria ranged from 80 to 180 leva, a staggering amount in view of the fact that monthly salaries varied from 350 to 700 leva.

At the time, I was in direct sales, and since vibrating belts of a popular brand had been actively advertised on TV, it was a solid reason to try them. After all, it was a trendy product and most people knew what the belts did and how to use them.

I found affordable belts of an unknown brand, which looked exactly like the expensive ones advertised on TV.

We were a team of three salespeople, actively engaged in direct sales and earning decent money. Or at least, decent in comparison to the salaries mentioned above. We worked every day, and spent late afternoons analyzing successes and failures. We moved on to new products each couple of months, or in case we found a more promising item than our current one.

We visited offices and sold our goods, or if we failed to make a sale, we tried to remember exactly what went wrong so that we could analyze it later. We juggled business coefficients and discussed them. Recounted different situations and outlined strategies so that we could get even better and more efficient. Things that few salespeople bother to do even today.

It was a Monday in September and people were busy; the holiday season had ended, and work processes were back to normal. Bobby and I went in an office building, intent on selling a belt or two. We took a look around and strategically targeted a woman slimmer than her coworkers. She was in fact the most slender one in the office.

Bobby introduced us. "Hello, we are volunteers in an anti-obesity campaign, and we're doing a survey. Can you please tell us how you keep in such excellent shape?"

The woman flushed a little at Bobby's compliment. "I don't think I'm in top shape, perhaps I need to lose some weight, but *I can't find the time to exercise.*"

That was one of our easiest chats; we had our clue in her very first answer, and we would use it later in the conversation.

"I think you look fantastic, and if you can spare five minutes of your time to fill in a survey, you'll win a great prize. What's your name?"

"Sure, why not. I'm Irena."

"Irena, are your cholesterol levels high?"

"I have no idea."

"Irena, how many hours of sleep do you get at night?"

"Well, I only sleep at night, usually 6 to 7 hours. Perhaps sometimes at the weekend I let myself sleep for 8." Irena laughed, as if she considered it the norm to sleep only at night and found our question a bit weird.

"I get why you laughed, but did you know that 30% of people find the time to sleep during the day, too?"

Our conversation drew attention, and two others joined us – a rather large woman and another one, who was not overweight, but definitely out of shape.

"How strange. And what's the reward I get for taking part in this survey?" Irena was growing restless. She obviously had her eyes on the prize, but she was probably expecting a key chain or some other small knick-knack.

"You already told us you don't exercise, but how many days a year you take off?"

"I use all of my twenty days off, going on holiday once in the summer and once in the winter."

Bobby asked Irena a few more questions and went for the kill. "Irena, thank you for your time. It's good you take active holidays, but you have to check your cholesterol levels and pamper yourself more. Your prize is a scented massage lotion or …" Bobby paused and turned to me. "Mate, those bargain vibrating belts, do we have any left?"

I confirmed we still had four.

"Irena, **as you already mentioned you had no time for exercise, but you wished you were even fitter and lost some weight**, I'll offer you this opportunity as well. You can buy one belt and get one more for free. You are in luck we still have a few left, today's the last day of our anti-obesity campaign."

"But why would I need two belts?"

"You can split the price with a coworker so that you both get a belt at half-price, or give the second one to someone, helping them improve their health (if we are dealing with a Yellow personality, they're already bought, because they always want to help and take care of their family).

Before giving the ladies the floor, Bobby mentioned a few of the belt's advantages, such as the ability to exercise while doing housework or watching TV; a morning routine for your belly and thighs while you brush your teeth; a ten-minute workout while doing the laundry or talking on the phone, etc.

While Bobby was talking about the belt, the large woman asked Irena to split the cost and get a belt each, since these belts were very popular now and quite expensive, so it was really a great opportunity.

It all worked out just the way we had planned.

The coworker was doing the persuading all on her own. She kept saying how popular these belts were, so the motivation to purchase was coming from her, too. And, instead of capitalizing on her eagerness to buy, we started to back away.

Bobby glanced at Irena and said, "We have to do several more surveys before lunch, so if you don't like our offer, just take the lotion. We should go, it's getting late."

Irena smiled at her colleague, and the lady seemed to have been waiting for this moment to take the lead. "I think we should take advantage of your offer. We plan on splitting the money."

Bobby looked at her, pursing his lips a little, and said, "You can take advantage if you do the survey first, because the name on the warranty card has to match the name on the survey."

"Sure, I'll do it."

And so, smiling and evidently in good spirits, the lady filled in the survey, and she and Irena got the great bargain. They bought a vibrating belt for 140 leva and got another one for free. It should be noted we'd purchased the belts wholesale for 27 leva each.

That was an exemplary deal: making excellent profit after following a perfect script.

Many dealers would have gone straight for the larger lady, but we'd found out it didn't yield such good results. If we introduced such a campaign to an overweight person, they might find it insulting. A slimmer person may take offence too, so our pitch to the more slender ones always ended with, "How do you maintain such excellent shape?"

Many dealers of the consultant variety would start by listing the belt's advantages and emphasizing what a good bargain it was. But again, it's not a very good approach, because it raises suspicion and clearly indicates that you are a seller going after profit.

Selling at a discount during an anti-obesity campaign is another thing entirely. Here, you're intent on helping people, and you offer a product designed to further your cause. The client can get a reward or take advantage of the offer, but only after doing a survey. This is a sale on condition, which is constructive because it shifts the focus from the sale to the person's health.

The survey provides an opportunity to have a short conversation with the prospective buyer and glean details of their life which they wouldn't share with a random salesperson who visited their office. Such a talk helps you gather clues that provide you with a script and a sales strategy – the way we learned that Irena wanted to lose weight, but couldn't spare the time, which was the most obvious sign we could have wanted. There were two of us, so that we could feed each other lines, and also, we sometimes visited offices with lots of people so we both needed to explain and sell.

Bobby's line, "Mate, do we have any bargain belts left?" was also not random. It showed the other party there was some bargain to be made, but it may be over, because these offers are always limited. Bobby claimed not to know since it was his job to conduct surveys, not sell belts. He was in a hurry to do his surveys, having a target to meet by lunchtime, and had no time to spare convincing people to buy something cheap. At the same time, he forced the clients' hand by limiting their time to react and make up their mind.

The fact that Irena's coworker took up the conversation, praising the belt's usefulness and popularity, was a stroke of luck. Unlike us, she had Irena's trust, and you are well aware that trust sells. At that point, another mechanism also went into play, namely uniformity.

Did you know that, if you asked your young kid to jump into a pool without a floaty, they would probably balk, but if they saw other kids their age jumping in there without floaties, the chance they tried it themselves would grow significantly.

That's exactly what happened in the office. One employee is much more likely to convince another than we ever would be. Most people assess the situation in the same way. The conversation triggers an automatic response and they buy, because we always see the world to our advantage and enjoy making great deals. We earn money to spend it, going shopping every day, and I doubt it anyone ever bought something under the impression that they were being cheated out of their money.

Everything we purchase is a bargain at that particular moment. Even buying a new car is a bargain.

They've given us a 5% discount, we're the very first owners, it's a unique feeling and we don't give a damn that as soon as we leave the store, the price of this car is already 30% lower, because we don't buy it to resell it. We buy it to drive it, love it and enjoy it.

One and the same offer, presented in different ways, may in some cases yield much better results. The good dealer and marketing expert's job is to construct the most successful strategy and steer events to a satisfactory ending.

SEVEN KEY FACTORS IN EFFECTIVE SALES AND PERSUASIVE COMMUNICATION

CURIOSITY/ FEAR/ ELATION/ SELFISHNESS/ TRUST/ POSSESSIVENESS/ EMOTIONAL ENGAGEMENT

A person can act just as impulsively out of fear as they would under the influence of elation or curiosity. Strategies in marketing and persuasive communication are often built upon any of these motivating factors.

Each message is aimed at eliciting an emotion, which in turn triggers consumers' urge to make a purchase.

When a person cuts themselves and knows it's nothing serious, they are not inclined to pay thousands to someone to clean the wound, administer a tetanus shot and put on a bandage. Of course, this holds true only if all other conditions are favorable. If the injury happened in the wilderness, cleaning the wound and taking the shot might be a question of life or death, and then a person would be willing to pay a lot, even parting with everything they had. So, we are ready to pay different amounts for the same product or service depending on the environment and the circumstances.

Everyone knows drinking beer at a bar costs much more than drinking it at home. In the first instance, we don't pay for the beer, but for the opportunity to drink it in a particular environment.

Remember, people are selfish by nature. Including those you approach directly at a dealer meeting or try to convince from a distance through advertising. These people do not care about your interests or your profit. They seek the best for themselves. Discounting this factor often leads to huge losses and wasted time and effort.

The difference between an advertisement and a salesperson is one of scale only!

I've often heard people claiming that advertisements aren't meant to sell, which I consider a sign of complete misunderstanding of the science of marketing. The difference between an advertisement and a salesperson is one of scale only! It speaks to thousands of people, while a salesperson to only one or a few at a time. That's why each advertisement should be a super-dealer and sell a lot. Communication shouldn't be reduced to several people talking face to face. Mastering it allows marketing experts and dealers to sell even from a distance.

If you found a whole bar of chocolate on the street, its packaging only slightly torn, would you eat it? Probably not. The fear of contagion and the surge of revulsion are much more powerful here than the spurt of happiness. You wouldn't eat it, because you can always go to the store and buy a new one. For a negligible amount, you could have that dose of elation whenever you want, so there's no need to take unnecessary risks.

However, if this bar was found by someone penniless, someone who hadn't eaten for days, they would be driven by elation and eat it without worrying about any risk of contagion. Living on the streets and searching the dumpsters for food, their life is a constant procession of risks: starvation, freezing, illness.

But imagine finding this chocolate bar and taking it to your office. If you left it on your desk and invited your coworkers to take a piece, they'd do so because they wouldn't know it was taken off the street, and they trust you.

People always see the world to their advantage. Have you ever heard of a guy hitting on a girl he's not attracted to, just for her sake, like "This girl is not much to look at, and I don't fancy her, but I'll start hitting on her and even marry her if she's up to it, just to indulge her!" or, if you are a woman, "Wow, what a plain boy, I don't like him in the slightest, but I want to see him happy."

Everyone cares about their own well-being first, and hopes their partner feels just as good with them. People often argue about what the other can't or won't do, about things that disrupt the comfort of either, because, as I already mentioned, we see everything to our advantage and are naturally selfish. Only Yellows do not possess this quality to such an extent.

If you tell a smoker to quit because one out of ten thousand smokers gets seriously ill and endangers their life, they won't care in the slightest. They'll give you an example of a non-smoker dying young or a person living to be 109 despite smoking two packs of unfiltered cigarettes a day. After all, the chance of it happening to them personally is trifling.

If you tell this same person that it's useless to buy lottery tickets because their chance of winning a serious prize is one in five million, they'll tell you that you can't win if you don't play. Many people have already won and changed their lives, so why can't they be among those too?

The odds don't matter. In the first instance, we deny the possibility of getting ill because we don't like it, so it needs not be true. In the second, we wish to be lucky and improve our way of life, so we are willing to waste money on something very unlikely to come true.

This is the very reason why advertisements calling for prevention and protection are much less successful than those selling hope and happiness:

» Companies manufacture beauty products but sell hope

» They print newspapers and magazines but sell hot news

» They make fruit juices but sell "natural" vitamins

» Dentists treat teeth but claim they produce smiles

» Patisseries bake cakes but sell delight

We can use all that to our advantage when we engage in negotiations or persuasive communication. When we'd like to evoke a need or replace an existing one with another suiting our purposes.

*Whether you are a salesperson or a marketing expert, you must be proficient in psychology, and the more proficient you are, the better, because **the world may change at great speed, but human psychology remains a constant**. Principles of psychology are clear cut and long-lasting. Ignoring or remaining unaware of them can only result in waste. In the waste of time and resources, in missed opportunities, and sometimes even in bankruptcy.*

In the examples that follow, I'm going to use the components of success – selfishness, curiosity, fear, elation, trust, possessiveness and emotional engagement, repeatedly. I'll keep explaining about personality colors and about the signs in the conversation, because they all are the key to the good results we all want for our businesses and for ourselves.

Some time ago, a marketing expert was tasked to boost the sales of a brand of toothpaste which was twice as expensive as the other brands offered at the time. He researched the paste's ingredients and benefits thoroughly, and after finding out more about dental plaque, which this paste removed better than the rest, he decided to pitch it as a beauty product, not as means to prevent dental problems like all other ads did. He tied plaque removal to acquiring beauty, not improving health. His campaign was a spectacular success because it had taken in consideration the fact that people see the world to their advantage and are selfish by nature. That we are guided by our dreams and the pursuit of happiness, not thinking about illness protection or things we don't like, thus denying they could happen to us. Nobody likes the prospect of their coming misery.

People are reluctant to pay for prevention, but are ready to give everything they have to cure themselves. They are unwilling to quit smoking despite the risks, but are eager to buy lottery tickets despite the miniscule chance of winning.

Salespeople have no desire to waste time researching the clients they plan to visit, but are content to stare at the float for hours without moving when they go fishing.

When we are somewhere we don't like to be, we're uneasy, and even a ten-minute wait can put us on edge. At the same time, we can lounge idly for hours elsewhere, claiming to be resting and relaxing.

We can't even handle brushing our teeth for two minutes and it's a burden, because many people consider it an obligation.

Since I'm constantly holding seminars in different cities and often have to travel around the country, during an intensive lottery advertising campaign, a friend of mine asked me to buy him a few tickets from every city or town I passed through, because he was convinced the winning ones were not in Sofia. Don't underestimate all these psychological factors. They are extremely important for good communication and effective deals. They play a role in the construction of every advertisement and even the formation of every company department. When you read about personality colors, I'm convinced you'll get many solutions to current problems or explanations about your past successes and failures. You'll be able to instantly recognize the dominating color of people around you.

I believe that what's written in this book will be of great help in your future dealer and marketing strategies, as well as in team motivation and management. But let's keep in mind that the better part of the book is dedicated to the power of persuasion.

STRATEGIC THINKING IN SALES

It was the fall of 1988, and in those times owning a color TV set was a privilege. Nice imported goods could be found only in the Korekom store, and the only currency they accepted was US dollars that few people could afford. Every kid's dream was owning a Lego set, but high marks in school were hardly enough to convince your parents to buy you the much coveted toy.

Peter was older than me, but we went to the same school and lived in the same building. We were good friends, played together and constantly sought each other's company.

His father used to travel abroad and awe us with his fascinating stories. One day, Peter brought me a present – bendy straws. I'd never seen one before. We had straws, but regular straight ones, while these were so beautiful: they could bend! I was sure everyone would be curious where they came from, and would like to own some.

Peter didn't have any Legos, and I had a very small set, but like all kids, we dreamed of owning a real large set of blocks, and these straws seemed like a great opportunity to achieve our goal. We came up with a strategy and Peter put it into action the very next day.

He brought the straws to school and told his classmates that his father had imported a machine for the production of such straws, but unfortunately, couldn't put it to use because he couldn't find suitable plastic. The children offered up different kinds of plastic packaging, yoghurt containers and so on, but Peter was quick to point out that they had tried it all and it didn't work.

A few days later, Peter came to school so excited you'd think he'd discovered America. "Guys, you won't believe it! We found the right plastic and we made some straws."

As he spoke, he started taking straws out of his bag. All kids got excited, and we achieved the desired effect. They all started questioning him what type of plastic it was, and he said he had tried with my Lego blocks and it worked. So he gave me five packets of straws in return, in front of everybody. Trembling with joy, I grabbed them and started jumping around.

The next day, there was already a line of school kids offering parts of their sets and expecting straws in return. Peter collected the blocks and brought them the straws the following day.

We collected so many blocks, there hardly existed a set so large.

But as with everything, this children's business affair also came to an end. The straws caused quite the ruckus at school, and parents of those children who had traded their Legos for straws complained to the teachers. So they called a parent-teacher conference, at which our trading strategy was unmasked and came to an abrupt end.

It came to light that Peter's father didn't own a straw-making machine; he had just imported large quantities of straws, intending to sell them. He hadn't known Peter had been taking straws and trading them for Lego blocks. Now he made Peter return it all to our schoolmates, which meant I had to give everything back, too. We were grounded, and the other kids got even more straws for free. But in spite of everything, it was then that I understood the power of strategic thinking and strategic sales.

When the children realized there was no machine and they'd been duped, they instantly lost interest in the straws. They wanted their Lego back and it again was worth more for them, while only a day ago we had made the objects switch values in favor of the straws.

If Peter had told everyone from the beginning that he had many straws, but no Lego, and was willing to trade straws for Lego blocks, hardly anyone would agree, not to mention exchange such quantities.

Remember, everything can be presented in different ways, and thus you can achieve better results with the same investment.

On the whole, we develop empirically, based on the principle of trial and error, which sets a barrier to our personal and career development. Those who manage to learn from their own mistakes and from those of others, grow much quicker.

I'll now share a sales strategy similar to the straw story, and very successful. It is yet another example of how one thing, presented in different ways, gets different results. Even the replacement of a single word in an ad can lead to a boost in sales.

The company I consulted catered to dentists, and wished to promote a new brand of dental burs (the small bits that fit in dental drills and are used to clean tooth cavities). They were top quality, made in Switzerland, but establishing yourself on this market was not an easy task despite the good reputation of the distributor company.

We organized promotional campaigns, one of which stated that if you buy ten burs, you get three for free. The company wasn't after huge profits but wanted a market share. The aim was to reach the dentists and induce them to buy, then we were sure that they will wish to continue working with the same product since it was really top quality.

Unfortunately, dentists are quite conservative and once they are used to working with specific equipment, they are rarely willing to replace it. The competition was fierce, and it was not easy to establish this product on the market despite our bargain offers and competitive prices.

We started giving away samples, convinced in their high quality, but another problem arose. During the sterilization process, our burs kept getting mixed with the others, and there was no way for the dentists to distinguish their better quality. The only way to make them see that we really had a top quality product, was to supply them with lots of burs and remove those of the competition.

Thus, knowing what we had to do and guided by psychology, we came up with our new sales strategy. We announced a limited period, during which we would buy out 50 old burs at the price of new ones, in case the dentist purchased 100 of our new burs. This in fact meant that, selling 100, we gave away 50 more, but we presented things differently. It was a sale on condition, which shifted the focus. Now it was all about buying out the old burs!

Imagine you had burs you'd used multiple times and they had to be replaced, and at one point someone offered to buy them at their original price. Someone offered to give you back the money you'd spent on those burs despite you using them multiple times and wearing them off, and in return, they asked that you buy 100 new ones. Sure, the quantities are huge, but it's a good bargain, don't you agree?

Many dentists took advantage of the deal, so we managed to sell them huge quantities and turn them into regular customers. Moreover, this approach had one more benefit that shouldn't be underestimated.

When we supply a client with such quantities, we eliminate the competition! How so? Because reps of competing companies would continue visiting the dentists regularly and offering them the same product they used to buy for a long time. But now it will be denied because the dentists still had a huge supply of it. Whatever offer the reps came up with in the next five to six months, it would be rejected, and that would make a dent in their motivation. And by the end of this period, the dentists would have gotten used to our burs' top quality at a very reasonable price, and would be unlikely to return to the old burs.

It's important to see the potential of a relationship, not just the profit from a one-time deal, like we did in this case.

The profit from this deal alone may not have been large. But in the future, these clients were going to order regularly, bringing considerable profit to the company in the long run – at the expense of their already eliminated competition.

EXPLOITING EMOTIONALLY-DRIVEN PURCHASES
TO INCREASE SALES BY 100%

A chain of pet stores was exactly like all the rest, selling pets and displaying a huge assortment of pet foods and accessories. They also offered vet services, but it still wasn't enough to make them stand out and boost their sales, because ordinary actions do not achieve extraordinary results.

They hired a sales and marketing expert who found a quick and easy-to-apply decision. He was well aware of the emotions driving potential clients to this kind of business, knew the power of possessiveness, and made a suggestion.

He suggested the company announce publicly that buying pet is a critical decision and should be well thought-out, so they offered their customers to take a cat or a dog home for a week or two, and if they found caring for them was not to their liking or seemed too hard, they could return the pet without paying a penny.

The offer appealed to many people who'd hesitated to buy their kids a pet, not sure what it would be like. But can you imagine returning a pet after your kid has cared for it a week or two? I believe you can either leave the pet home or send your child off along with it.

Emotional engagement plays a huge part here as well; it's a key factor to consider in effective sales and persuasive communication.

This strategy led to an impressive increase in sales and made the pet store chain stand out, which is yet another proof that strategic thinking can improve results even without huge investments and expensive marketing activities.

People today have too varied a choice, more so than ever, coupled with too little time to come to a decision. It makes us decide primarily on the basis of trust – and trust requires excellent communication.

Nobody likes being sold to, but everybody likes buying! That's why a good salesperson should provide their current and potential customers with an opportunity to strike a bargain, fashioning all advertising slogans and marketing activities accordingly.

THE SENSE OF POSSESSION – MORE IMPORTANT THAN THE SALE ITSELF

When you are engaged in a product business not involving or not limited to distance sales, then your potential clients must have physical access to your product.

Perhaps you're saying, and so what, it's only natural. It's natural, sure, but its potential is not always taken into account or used to its best advantage.

We've all seen how laptops are arranged in most computer and electronics stores – with the top partially closed or fully open, but at such an angle that it's impossible to see well what's on the screen. Of course, they must also be switched on and in working mode. Thus, when a person wants to take a look, they have to position the device closer to themselves and adjust the top in order to see better, and then, possibly, try it out. These actions immediately evoke a sense of possession, and today this sense is considered more powerful than the sale itself.

Many people only readjust the position of the screen in order to see the image better, without touching the laptop any further. Few realize, and perhaps many of you wouldn't even believe it, but lots of studies show that the sense of possession has a significant impact on sales – of course, a favorable one.

Well-trained salespeople give customers the opportunity to browse the web, watch a DVD or play a game, because it creates a sense of possession.

Consultants often demonstrate what a product can do without allowing customers to touch it, and when the demonstration is over, they offer the audience to buy it. That's not recommended in cases when the customer could actually interact with the product.

Lots of fashion stores provide the opportunity to buy products and try them at home, then return those that don't fit or appeal without the need for explanation. I hope you don't think they do themselves a disservice by trying to indulge the client.

In Bulgaria, not all stores are willing to give you your money back if you buy something as a gift and are not sure whether it will be appreciated. Best case scenario, they will allow you to replace it with something of higher or equal value. Such restrictions don't achieve anything and are by no means beneficial to the potential customer relationship, which should be a priority of every business. **Restrictions diminish potential!**

Try visiting a store and saying you want to buy five pairs of shoes so your friend can choose one, and you'll return the rest in a week or two. I'm almost sure nobody will oblige you. Or at least, nine out of ten stores will not. Such wishes would be considered pure whim, let alone if you asked to try out ten pairs.

Few people realize that trying something out is an advantage, not a disadvantage.

In a huge international chain of shoe stores there was a rule: after a customer chose a particular pair and decided to buy, they should be offered five additional pairs to try out without being obliged to buy any of them. If the customer accepted, they received a 5% discount for the pair they'd already decided on.

This approach led to an increase in sales. As it turned out, one in seven customers bought a second pair of shoes, and one in fifty bought a second and a third.

At the basis of this strategy for boosting sales lies the sense of possession.

Thanks to the additional discount of 5%, the strategy became a huge success. I only forgot to mention, the customers agreeing to try out five more pairs to get their discount, had to try pairs given by the staff, not ones they chose themselves.

Now you are probably wondering how the staff could know which model would suit the client better than the clients themselves.

In retail stores, strategic sales involve the constant collecting of consumer data related to clients' behavior and interests.

One of the reasons to employ a loyalty program is, it provides the opportunity to gather lots of information (business coefficients) about your customers, which you can later use strategically. Every time a client purchases or returns a product, they have to log their card, allowing the program to update their file.

With minimal effort, you can access a client's history at any time. To see what they bought, whether they took advantage of promotional campaigns, discounts and clearance sales. Whether they reacted to the emails you sent out and to the attempts at cross-selling. You can monitor their purchase frequency, the average money they spend, the overall amount spent throughout the previous year, the number of purchases, when they had last visited the store before their current visit, and so on. All extremely important information.

All that, combined with a well-trained and highly motivated staff, allowed the salespeople at the store to offer a client five pairs of shoes they would most probably like.

If clients had to choose those pairs by themselves, they could try out five random pairs just for show, try out something unorthodox out of curiosity or waste much of the staff's time deliberating which shoes to choose.

If the client was Green, they could easily take up too much of the salespeople's time, wanting details about each model and weighing up possibilities. Or if the client was Blue, which means never in a hurry and extremely talkative, choosing each pair might be accompanied by an interesting story. Both of which no business can afford because they are too far from the goal, i.e. numerous and effective sales.

That's why it was the staff's decision what the customer should try out, based on information about their previous behavior, or in case there was no such information, it was all up to the salesperson's competence and their excellent understanding of people.

Usually, the client got five pairs very similar to the one they'd decided to buy – as long as the shoes were not bought as a gift, which you have no way of knowing if you don't talk with the client. Communication is extremely important. The likelihood of them taking to one of the five pairs was high, and if they hesitated whether to buy it, they got a stimulating discount of 10% for the second pair. After purchasing it too, they received yet another discount, this time 20%, if they decided on buying a third pair.

Or as they say, keep offering until the client says "enough". If we focus on relationship potential, we shouldn't be aggressive and overwhelm customers, led by the idea that once they're here, it's our chance to strip them of all their money. That said, we still should make a few strategic offers and attempt cross-selling, if the business allows it. If you'd like to know more about what cross-selling entails, I'll tell you about that extremely profitable strategy later in the book.

Perhaps you're wondering whether there was a sign on the store front or elsewhere, announcing these discounts and opportunities? No, they were not posted anywhere, and were offered only at the staff's discretion. It's not always the right time to make such offers, because this approach could be unsuccessful on occasion. It matters how things are going in the store, how busy it is and how many salespeople are available to interact with customers.

At rush hours, when a store is overflowing with customers and everyone seeks additional information and assistance, it's not a good time to make offers aimed at expanding the purchase. In such circumstances, the time available for serving a single client drops down, so you can only afford a quick cross sale at the cash deck area and no more.

During busy periods, prolonged attention to a single client will most likely mean lack of any attention to another, which can lead to the loss of said client. And as you can imagine, it's much more important not to lose customers and to have everyone happy, than to expand sales and increase the average amount spent.

After reading about this strategy, I guess you can think of various ways to implement it in the business you are currently running, or in your future business enterprise.

You are well aware that all car dealers constantly encourage their customers to go for test drives, and the reason is not that they want to run down a car or two and then sell them at a reduced price, but they are well aware that the sense of possession and emotional engagement are both key weapons in the arsenal of persuasive communication.

STRATEGIC SALES:
SELLING A NEW CAR

Ivan worked as a consultant in a new car dealership, and his job was to answer clients' requests daily and consult those who came to the showroom in person.

The showroom door opened and in came a man of average height, humbly dressed. Yet another of the day's customers. The empty room obviously made him nervous. He appeared soon after everybody had returned from lunch break, when business was usually slow, and that gave Ivan the opportunity to have a leisurely, unhurried chat with him. But before introducing himself, he gave the client a minute to walk around and get accustomed to his surroundings.

As the client was examining one of the cars, Ivan engaged in what he did best: selling. "Hello, sir, my name is Ivan Kiryakov and I'm a sales consultant. May I assist you while you're browsing?" Ivan offered his hand.

The man timidly took it, introducing himself. "I'm Steve, Steve Krastev." At the time, Mr. Krastev was examining a low-end model.

"Mr. Krastev, can you spare me twenty minutes of your time? If you can, I believe I have a very nice surprise for you."

"I do have the time, but please tell me, what's this about?"

"Please follow me, Mr. Krastev." Ivan led Mr. Krastev to the back exit where a real beast was waiting, packing 370hp under its hood at the cost of a small apartment.

"Ivan, that's not for me, I'm looking for something entirely different."

"I understand, Mr. Krastev, but we've never had such a car for test driving before, so I'd very much like to try it out. While driving around, you can tell me what it is you're looking for. I don't expect you to buy this car, just get in and drive it a bit, come on."

"Oh no, you drive, please. I'm afraid to handle this monster, something may happen."

Ivan saw that the client was nervous and didn't press him. He just invited him to the passenger seat and their trip began. "Mr. Krastev, I'd very much like to have a car like this someday, but it won't be any time soon. We'd just had a second child and I must be more practical, so I've set my eye on a family vehicle. Do you have kids?"

"I do, two boys of five and eight."

"That's wonderful, I wish them all the best. I'd like to have a boy too, but we'll hardly try for a third child. We have two girls now, a four-year-old and a few-months-old."

"Never mind that, Ivan, as long as they're happy and healthy."

During the short drive, Ivan managed to glean many more things about Steve, namely, that he enjoyed camping, fishing, family hikes and traveling as a whole. He also learned that Steve held a managerial, but not very well-paid position in a small company that imported and traded fast-moving consumer goods, and that his current car needed replacing. But just like many others, Steve hadn't picked a particular brand or model, just compared options and collected offers.

Less than ten minutes later, the two of them were again in the showroom, chatting like old friends.

Steve asked Ivan to go back to the car he had examined in the beginning, perhaps it was the kind of car he could afford. "What do you think of this car, Ivan?"

"Steve, I'll let the car speak for itself. A person wishes to try out a new pair of shoes before buying it, let alone when it's such an expensive purchase. If you have thirty more minutes to spare, I'll have this model available for a test drive. My colleague currently took another client in it. And while we wait, we can do a turn in one of our family vehicles. A unique minivan, a personal favorite of mine."

Steve now felt more comfortable, Ivan was a pleasant companion who smiled a lot and didn't pressure him in the slightest. So Steve accepted the offer immediately, his initial nervousness gone. The two went once more to the back entrance, where the van waited, equipped with all the extra features of the model except leather upholstery. It glistened in the sun and had that new car smell.

"Steve, you're driving this time. Don't worry, nothing bad can happen. Believe me, you won't be held responsible for anything."

Steve raised his eyebrows, let out a loud sigh as if he was expected to do the impossible, and held his hand to Ivan for the keys. Then he smiled and got in the van. "It really looks great, Ivan."

"I told you, Steve, that's the car I've been waiting for. It'll soon be mine. I've got insight info that there's going to be a promotional campaign next month. Five of these vans will be offered at a huge discount and I'm intent on buying one. Another colleague is also buying, and we're keeping the rest for friends. The model you liked will also be on offer next month, with a free set of winter tires or full insurance, whichever you prefer. But let it stay between us, or they'll be kicking me out of here in no time flat."

Steve drove, looking lost in thought, just like Ivan had expected. "Ivan, that van is great, it would be just perfect for us."

"Yeah, Steve, who wouldn't want this baby?"

"How much is it?"

"Oh, it's more costly than the one you had your eye on. That's why I've been waiting for a year for this offer – it'll save me a ton of money, even with my employee discount I wouldn't get half that amount off."

"And still, how much is it?"

"Hey, Steve, so you are not 100% sure about the little guy?"

"No, I'm not. It really is a bit too small for a family car. But it's practical. I haven't made up my mind yet."

"Steve, I've been selling cars for ten years and I can assure you, family cars are the most practical. Let me explain. Small cars are city cars. They're often bought for company vehicles or young drivers. They are more fuel-efficient, cheaper to maintain, and that's it. Luxury models are bought for prestige, that's obvious. And family cars are most sought after by end consumers, and the competition is fierce. I've researched many brands and models and this is an exceptional car, and at the coming discount it would be without rivals."

"You're right, I guess."

Ivan skillfully drove the conversation away from the price. It was too early to talk money, not before the client fell in love with the vehicle.

Steve fell silent, and a few minutes later they again parked by the showroom. Ivan, losing no time, grabbed the keys and papers for the lower-end model, and invited Steve on yet another test drive. "Come on, Steve, let's try out your pick."

Steve didn't refuse and got in the car, but it was obvious he didn't enjoy the drive and didn't feel fond of the vehicle – one that only thirty minutes earlier he had intended to buy.

"Steve, you know it's my job to sell cars. I think *this* car is definitely not right for you. You said you had two kids, so it will be too small, and I can see you don't seem to like it. Perhaps it's better you looked elsewhere."

"To be honest, I liked the van a lot."

"And the first car, didn't you like that one too?" Ivan smiled and patted Steve on the shoulder.

"Sure I did, but it's far out of my league."

"Hey, Steve, let me do something for you. If you really liked the van, I'll patch you up with the coming offer. I'll tell you when to come for the advance payment, and leave the rest to me. I told you there'll be five cars on offer, we've set aside four. I'll tell the others I'm reserving the last one for yet another friend, but I'll ask you for a favor in return."

"What favor?"

"I'd like you to send a letter of thanks to me, to my boss's email. I've been planning on asking for a raise for some time, and I need a trump-card. Would you help me?"

Steve smiled and said he was going to send such a letter anyway, he was so pleased with Ivan.

While they were parking the car, Steve asked about the exact cost of the van with the discount Ivan was going to take advantage of.

"Steve, I can't tell you right now. Remember, the offer is not out yet. If you want, tell me what features you'd like for your van to have, and I'll send you an unofficial email from my personal account. But please don't call at the office asking for any details, they'll chuck me out in a blink."

And just like that, Steve was swept into a conspiracy. He had come at the right time and stumbled upon the right consultant. In a month, he would be able to take advantage of a unique offer for a select few. Of course he would keep it to himself; after all, if Ivan fell out of favor, Steve would miss the offer, too.

"Steve, think it through, it's a serious purchase. Whatever information you need, you can count on me, but please don't buy that little guy. Each new car is being driven for at least five years, and if you don't feel at ease or it doesn't offer the comfort you've been dreaming of, you've sabotaged yourself, man. Think it through."

Steve already knew he wouldn't buy the small car; he was more worried about how he was going to pay for the van and whether Ivan would really fix him up with the fabled discount. Ivan knew it too, so he kept stripping value of the low-end model and fawning over the van.

It all followed Ivan's script; a month later, Steve had already provided the advance payment and waited for his new van. Ivan had been delivered a bottle of good whiskey, and his boss received yet another appreciative email, in which Steve had stated brief and clear how happy he was with Ivan's service and expertise, and how he wished all consultants were like him.

Ivan's boss, Joro, went down the stairs, grinning and holding a sheet of paper. Tilting his head to the side, he glanced at Ivan. Then he shook his head and said, "How do you do it, pal? Getting gifts and thank-you letters after each sale. How do you manage it? Hey, guys, that's yet another appreciative letter from a client, I'm putting it up on the board. Read it and weep."

What Ivan was, was a professional dealer. He was exactly who his clients needed him to be. And his clients were always lucky. They always bought the very last cars available or were given special discounts. Ivan was an excellent judge of character and used a different approach each time.

What can we learn from this story?

– It's better not to approach customers the second they set foot in the store. The client doesn't feel comfortable inside until they're at least ten feet in and had spent more than ten seconds there. So wait them out, give them a little time to take in their surroundings, and then engage them.

– Nine out of ten clients, if asked "How can I help you?" or "Can I be of service?", reply with "Just looking around." That's why Ivan asked Steve "May I assist you with your browsing?" Phrased like that, the question cannot be refuted with "Just looking around", and the likelihood of the client accepting your offer increases by a hundredfold. Because what can you do if to your "Can I be of service?", you receive a "No, I'm just looking around"? Of course, that shouldn't be a problem either, because truth is, **the salesperson's work begins when the client says no**. But Ivan's strategy in this particular case is definitely a winner.

– Don't introduce yourself to every customer if you own a store selling mass-produced, fast-moving consumer goods. These are totally different businesses and require different sales strategies.

– When Ivan asked Steve whether he had twenty minutes to spare, he piqued his curiosity with an element of surprise; something nice he would miss if he said he had no time. Thus he takes away Steve's opportunity to say he was in a hurry. If you asked a client whether they had time to spare without adding the element of surprise, over 70% would answer in the negative. If you included an allusion to a nice surprise, less than 30% would claim they had no time.

– The reason for getting into the luxury vehicle was again strategic. While they were traveling in the car that held no appeal for Steve, there was no reason for their talk to focus on the car. These ten minutes spent in the high-end car provided Ivan with the perfect ambience to glean valuable information about his client.

Ivan didn't take the client to test the car he wanted right away, because that car was a low-end model, and **a key principle in sales is to start out with the expensive products and move to cheaper ones**.

When you present a high-end product, all those that follow are lower-end and respectively, cheaper. Whereas if you start with a bargain one, the price will only go up. This is a matter of psychology which should be taken into account, as it is perceived as the golden rule in sales.

During their drive, Ivan mentioned he'd been a car dealer for ten years, which meant he knew the market and the competition well. Then Ivan explained that family cars were most cost-effective in numerous respects. Each piece of information was carefully gauged. Many dealers would say directly, "Let me tell you what to buy" or "I've been in this business for ten years, you should listen to me", and so on. But that's not the right approach. Demonstrating authority and forcing your point of view on the customer in such a blunt and straightforward manner rarely achieves good results. And arguing with your client is an absolute no-no in strategic sales and persuasive communication.

Now's the time to mention that the moment a client has an objection, expresses their doubts in a product or compares it to that of a rival company, many dealers fail, taking it too personally. The client's reaction hurts their ego, and things rarely end in a deal.

The truth is, objections often come from interested customers. Sometimes those having objections are in fact the only ones buying. An objection should be considered a sign of interest and be welcomed, not reviled.

I'll repeat yet again that people see the world to their advantage, and Ivan used this predisposition of ours to guarantee his deal. He off-handedly mentioned the coming promotional campaign without offering Steve to take advantage of it. Rather, he shared his own intention to cash in on the offer, which led Steve to muse why a car dealer would consider buying a family van, which is not a high-end vehicle. His curiosity and envy were aroused, and his selfishness exploited.

It was said the offer had been awaited for a year, and it was obviously a great one, if the discount was twice the one given to employees. Everything was made to sound extremely appealing without mentioning any numbers.

Numbers often draw the attention, making people focus on them more than on the rest of the conversation. So you must shift the focus and make the client follow the conversation and engage in it, not be a passive listener.

Remember something very important: *People don't dream about things they can afford. It is those things outside our means that we set our sights on.*

Before telling you another story, a shorter one recounting how Ivan sold his old car, I'd just like to point out that persuasive communication and marketing are part of our everyday lives. Sometimes we apply them successfully without even noticing.

When you wish to sell your car, you wash it, doll it up, and cover up the obvious defects, if possible. Clean the inside, and then put an ad with an alluring message, hoping to attract potential customers and broker a sale. This is all marketing.

Now let me tell you how Ivan sold his used car, using quite the opposite approach.

STRATEGIC SALES:
SELLING A SECOND-HAND CAR

Ivan's car had a lot of surface defects, it had been in a light accident and needed repairs he didn't intend to do. The car was eight years old and Ivan knew very well that from now on, the need for repairs would only grow.

He carefully analyzed all the ads on a leading website for second-hand car sales, read through the information they provided, studied the pictures, and came up with his strategy.

Ordinary actions do not lead to extraordinary results. Ivan knew that very well, and he realized it was pointless to do what all the others did.

After polishing the car's interior to within an inch of its life and upholstering the wheel with brand new leather, he took photos of the car, some of which clearly showed where the paint was scratched, which was entirely deliberate.

He composed a description, explaining in detail all that has been done to the car; the interior was like new because it had been well cared for, and the surface defects were not removed deliberately, so that the car could be seen in its true condition, since each paint job aroused doubts in potential customers. He also said that the price took into account the car's condition, and added, "I'm no car dealer. I'm selling this car because I'm about to buy a new one." If you are wondering about the price, it was one of the highest for this brand and model. Much sleeker cars, looking like new, were selling for less. But Ivan's description did its job.

Ivan didn't expect to sell the car at that price, but was aware that whatever the price was, the buyer would try to lower it, and also, that people associated high prices with high quality.

His ad definitely confused people, because the car didn't look like much, but was among the most expensive. He had to knock a couple of thousand off to go closer to its actual price, at which he intended to close the deal. Of course, that was only part of his strategy; here comes the most curious part.

A day after the ad was posted, the first potential client called. "Hello, I'm calling for the car ad."

"Hello sir, sorry I haven't removed the ad, but the car is sold."

"How strange that you managed to sell it so fast. I check the ads every day; this one was posted yesterday, and today, the car is sold. You're very lucky."

"The truth is, the car was in excellent condition, sir. I offered a man to trade it up for his almost new one, and after he examined it at a repairs shop and made sure it really was first-rate and all its defects were only superficial, he agreed to a trade-up. I made up the difference."

"Was he going to sell it or drive it?"

"Oh, sell it, by all means. He was just finding it difficult to sell his own car, so after I offered him a significant amount, he decided it would be much easier to take the deal and sell my car instead. The man even said that he was planning to patch it up and ask a lower price than mine, because he didn't want to wait. Between you and me, he said if someone offered him 8,000 leva, they'd get it right away."

"Okay, now that you've gotten rid of it, would you at least tell me what its actual condition was?"

"Sure – it really was excellently looked after." And so Ivan told the potential client how great the car was and how it was very much worth it, but most people were fools and bought cars with the odometers rolled back and all signs of accidents covered up to appear like brand new.

Then, at the client's request, he provided the new owner's number. This "new" owner, Emil Kostadinov, was a friend of Ivan's and didn't mind helping with the sale.

Only ten minutes later, Emil's phone was ringing, and it was the same number. The client called Emil, probably hoping that the car would be still available and he could really buy it at the lower price cited by Ivan. "Hello, I'm interested in this car ..." The client mentioned the brand and model, but didn't tell Emil he knew everything about the car form its "previous" owner – Ivan.

"Yes, it's for sale." And Emil cited a price with 1,000 leva higher than the one Ivan had mentioned. And of course, lower than the one in Ivan's original ad.

"Okay, where can I look the vehicle over?"

So Emil and the client arranged to meet. The client went with the clear intention not to look the car over, since he was already convinced it was excellent, but to bargain about the price until they agreed on the 8,000 Ivan had mentioned. He had no idea Emil and Ivan were friends and that Emil knew exactly what was going to happen.

So when they met, Emil somehow reluctantly knocked off the requested amount and they closed the deal.

He received the exact price Ivan wanted with ease, thanks to their excellent strategy.

If you are wondering what would happen when the buyer saw the car's papers and realized its registration card was old and the car hadn't changed owners, I'll tell you. Emil had a letter of attorney and everything was as it should be. There were hundreds of ads featuring cars in the same condition and at similar prices, which remained unnoticed for months.

Now some of you may call this a scam, not a clever sale. But I don't believe deceit has any place in sales whatsoever.

Professional dealers never lie; they may twist things a little, may present them in a totally different light, may spare some fine points and details, but shouldn't lie.

Salespeople are no liars.

Think about it. After all, it's a deal between the owner and the customer. No fraud here. The customer doesn't buy anything different than what he'd been promised. The car's mileage is correct and its appearance is not perfect, and he can see it. It doesn't look like a car he would buy. But the deal is not forced on him, he's entirely willing to do it.

In this deal, the focus was shifted to the possible cheaper price, while the car's appearance and outer condition were ignored.

The only fabrication is the trade-up, but it in no way affects the car's actual characteristics. It is, no doubt, a manipulation and a fib, but luckily an entirely harmless one.

I say harmless, just like all foodstuffs should be safe and contain no harmful ingredients. All their ingredients are listed on the label, but it never says that too great quantities of a certain ingredient may present a serious risk for your health.

Important: *Everything is a matter of dosage! Let's not overdo the amount of fibs in our sales strategies, thus causing consumers to come to harm. Let's stay professional. You are well aware that any medicine, taken in too large a dose, may become poison!*

I guess you are now all too eager to know about personality colors. I won't be surprised if you've already browsed forward and read about their basic characteristics; after all, curiosity is a key factor in sales and persuasive communication.

If you still haven't, I'll tell you one more story about a strategic sale, and right afterwards, I'll share all about personality colors.

In the following story about the strategic sale of a home-cleaning machine, you'll witness yet again how powerful persuasive communication can be. Let's see how you can sell expensive cleaning equipment, designed to do an excellent job of washing your floors and furniture, but at a shocking price in comparison with similar products offered at retail stores.

STRATEGIC SALES:
SELLING A HIGH-END HOUSE CLEANING MACHINE

How many customers can afford a modern vacuum cleaner with integrated cleaning, washing-up and drying features at a cost of several thousand?

If you believe that only wealthy people could, and that they are too small a target group, then you've learned nothing. To sell such a piece of equipment to either an affluent customer or to one of humbler means, it is required to utilize some of the elements of persuasive communication that you read about so far.

If in the past it was sufficient to ring the doorbell and offer a free demonstration, and then be convincing enough to make the person want this miracle of technology – which can be theirs for only 100 leva a month for a three-year period, and with a down payment of 800 leva – today, it's much more complicated. Everybody employs the same approach, so it has gradually stopped being effective and no longer achieves the desired results.

Martin's task was to help the dealers reach more households, where they could make their demonstration and convince the family to buy this miracle that could save them from dust, dirt and microbe-infested air.

Martin knew the solution must be outside the routine approach, so he had to find another, better working strategy.

After analyzing some of the people who had already bought the excellent house cleaning machine, a plan started forming in Martin's head, and it would soon evolve into an effective means of finding potential customers.

– What do the dealers want? – More meetings and preliminary information about the household.

– Who are those potential customers? – People who insist on cleanliness, who have children, try to lead a healthier lifestyle, care about the environment, are not fond of traditional medicines but trust homeopathy, ride bikes, practice sports, etc.

– Would you let in a random stranger ringing the doorbell? – People are wary and won't let just anyone in, so we take no for the standard answer.

– If you receive a call offering a demonstration at your home, would you accept? – Most people would recognize the demonstration as an attempt to sell them something. People don't like being sold to, they like buying.

These are some of the questions Martin used as a foundation for his strategy, which you will see in the following paragraphs. I believe it will be of help when you construct your own future strategies.

As a business coach, I ask lots of questions to my clients daily, and I witness their extraordinary progress. I see their tremendous personal improvement and business growth. Questions are keys to new opportunities. Use them!

Martin decided to do a phone survey aiming to gather crucial preliminary information about potential customers, which would later make his colleagues' work easier. But who would answer the questions of a phone survey and why would they?

He had to motivate people to do so, so if they agreed to spare a minute answering a few questions, their names would be entered in a raffle where every other one won.

And that was not all.

The winners would be those who gave suitable answers, and the price would be the cleaning of an entire room and the furniture within with the machine in question. Thus, one survey could be the answer to all the challenges that Martin had to deal with.

So here's how Martin put his strategy to use and turned it into a valuable resource for effective sales.

Call #1: sample conversation with a potential client

"Hello, my name is Martin and I'm calling from Herzenburg. We're doing a survey aimed at improving the quality of life in Bulgaria. If you can spare a minute to answer a few questions, you can also win a prize. Every other entry wins, but even if you don't, you'd have helped a good cause."

"Hello. So, what's this survey about?"

"Would you tell me, in your opinion, do you lead a healthy life, or not so much?

"I believe it is healthy, but I know it could be even more so."

"Where do you live?"

"Sofia."

"Do you suffer from high blood pressure?"

"No, I have no medical conditions."

"Would you tell me, how old are you?"

"Forty-six."

"Do you measure the humidity levels in your home and do you know what the recommended levels for a bedroom are?"

"No, I've never thought about it."

"How often do you eat out?"

"At least once a day."

"Do you consume instant foods at home?"

"No."

"Do you live in your own place, or rent one?"

"My own, but it's mortgaged."

"How many members does your household consist of, and what's your role?"

"It's four of us, I'm a wife and a mother of two."

"Last question, madam. What is your floor covering, do you have carpets or rugs?

"Yes, the floors are tiled or laminated, but we also have floor carpeting and rugs in some rooms."

"Thank you very much for your time, we'll be in touch if you win a prize. Do you have any questions? And would you please tell me your name so that I can enter you in the raffle?"

"Yes, what's the point of this survey? My name's Nicoletta."

"Nicoletta, the point is to improve the quality and the average life expectancy in the country. More and more children are suffering from asthma-related conditions and allergies, especially those living in big cities such as yours."

"All right, that's a great initiative. Good luck."

"Thank you again for your time, Nicoletta. Have a nice day."

"Thank you, you too."

I'm sure you have questions and objections towards some parts of this interview, but let's have a closer look at it.

Why did Martin skip the classic opener demonstrating good manners, i.e. "Is it all right to talk?"

This question drastically reduces the number of successful outcomes, because people often say "No, now's not a good time" or ask what it was about and before you manage to explain, they hang up or excuse themselves. On the other hand, why would someone pick up with an unknown number calling, if it wasn't a good time? That's the reason why Martin didn't start with "Is it all right to talk?", even if that is considered an example of good manners. Instead, he said all the important stuff and hoped to invoke curiosity. There were two provocative phrases: a good cause and a prize for every other entrant.

The person on the phone could refuse, because they were given the opportunity and didn't feel hard-pressed.

And if you worry about honesty, in this particular case the fabrication is negligible and rather harmless. Using this machine would really improve people's quality of life, and everyone who used it at least once is extremely satisfied and does not feel deceived in the slightest.

The only fib is the involvement in a good cause, but why consider it a fib: it could be called a good cause when the result is improving people's quality of life, right?

Everything is a play on words, there's no deceit, unlike those cock-and-bull stories we hear in TV ads of food supplements, cleaning supplies or magnetic belts treating pain of unknown origin, most likely caused by a slipped disc.

"The difference between the almost right word and the right word is really a large matter – 'tis the difference between the lightning bug and the lightning."
–Mark Twain

The conversation goes on, and different recipients can be asked different questions depending on answers provided, gender and age.

In the answers, Martin and his colleagues track different personality traits and group people according to certain criteria, which will help them measure the effectiveness of this initiative. And a day or two later, there comes a second call. The call shouldn't be delayed more than a couple of days because otherwise there's a strong possibility that the person on the other end will no longer remember the previous conversation and the survey.

Call #2 – a sample conversation with a potential client

"Hello, Nicoletta, Martin calling. Exactly two days ago you spared us some of your time to complete a survey, and I'm happy to inform you that you are among the winners of our raffle. Do you remember our conversation?"

"Yes, hello. What did I win?"

"The prize is free professional cleaning of a room in your home and all the furniture inside. The cleaning will be done with the most modern equipment, you won't believe the results, I'm sure. It will happen at a time that is convenient for you, and our consultant will also give you valuable advice for a healthier lifestyle. When are you available?"

"Sounds great, but it won't be necessary to buy something or pay for the service, correct?"

"Oh no, it's completely free of charge. We'll only ask you to sign the survey you completed on the phone, so that we can file it with our German partners. Is it okay for my colleague to come on Thursday at 7 p.m.?"

"Yes, I think so. How long would the procedure take?"

"It usually takes about half an hour. But we won't be in a hurry to leave and will answer all your questions, because I'm sure you'll have some."

"Okay, Thursday at 7 it is."

This was Martin's strategy, which helped him gather preliminary information and turned the demonstration into a prize.

Being called and offered free cleaning is quite different from winning one.

Think about it – why should someone offer you free cleaning? It's clear there's a catch, and it's obviously going to be a demonstration. The probability of rejecting such an offer is much greater.

Yes, some people refuse the prize because they realize it's a demonstration, but many others accept it, and a considerable number of them buy the unique machine.

During the demonstration itself, people see dirt they didn't even suspect existed, an in their own home no less.

They realize the air is not fresh enough, and it constitutes a risk for them and their children. Their fears are awoken, and they suddenly become a strong enough drive to purchase.

Some things cannot be sold from a distance, or at least not as successfully as after face-to-face communication. This machine is one of those products where people buy health and fresh air enriched with negative ions, as if you lived by the Niagara Falls.

Now, at last, we come to the chapter on personality colors. I'd like to point out in advance that this is my own interpretation, based on nearly twenty years in sales and on the analyses of thousands of meetings.

Like any salesperson who wishes to improve their skills, for many years I would record my meetings on a portable tape recorder, and then spend a few hours each night analyzing them, looking for the signs and trying to improve my skills.

To be good in this field, you have to invest a lot in self-improvement, which inevitably involves lots of hard work and rough times, exactly like any other responsible and difficult vocation.

PERSONALITY COLORS
AND THEIR RESPECTIVE TRAITS

DIFFERENT PERSONALITY TYPES AND HOW TO SPEAK THEIR LANGUAGE

Even before the beginning of the Current Era Hippocrates classified people in four basic personality types:

Sanguine individuals – highly responsive, reacting to anything that attract their attention. Very energetic and hard-working. Characterized by quick movements and fast speech. Quick to engage strangers. Easily get used to new environments and adapt their habits. Balanced.

Choleric individuals – similar to the sanguine, but more violent, hot-tempered, impatient and uncontrolled. Unbalanced.

Phlegmatic individuals – characterized by underdeveloped emotionality, bland movements. Exhibit patience and self-possession. Slow to move, slow to focus and difficult to switch gears. Find it difficult to engage strangers, to change their habits and adapt to new surroundings. Balanced.

Melancholic individuals – easily offended and highly sensitive. Very shy and self-doubting. Even an insignificant difficulty can make them give up. Easily tired, not energetic and not particularly hard-working.

Besides Hippocrates, personality types were classified also by Jung, who divided people into extroverts and introverts, Sheldon, who differentiated between endomorphs, ectomorphs and mesomorphs, and other researchers, Ernst Kretschmer and Ivan Pavlov among them.

For the purposes of persuasive communication and effective sales, it's important to understand people and know how to speak their language, so that we are able to motivate and/or manipulate them. That's why we'll divide them into four basic colors: blue, green, yellow and red. This way, their characteristics will be easier to remember, and we'll learn more easily how to communicate and work with them. Most people are a combination of these colors, but there is always one standing out – the predominant color.

You can come up with your own classification of people to make them easier to remember and deal with. A piece of advice: don't divide them in more than four groups, because they'll become exceedingly difficult to differentiate in the process of working.

Quite a few years ago, when I decided to take notes and attempt a serious analysis of consumer behavior, I distinguished between eight personality types, which in time I reduced to six, and later, after the advice of a mentor of mine, transformed into the current four types.

Since I'm guessing you'll start immediately analyzing yourself and your family after reading about the types, don't try to see them as a single color only. Such people are rare. Look for the predominant color, because most people are a combination of several.

When we find out a person's predominant color, we'll know how to act around and talk to them. Once we've discovered their personality type, we'll be able to attract their attention, motivate them and make them do what we want, using manipulation techniques tailored to their respective color.

REDS

They love to be in charge, to command, organize and control people. Responsible and ambitious. Fond of money and not interested in much else. Capable of earning a lot, but, just like Blues, not very attentive, because they are convinced they already know everything.

These people are natural competitors, love challenges and are willing to win at all costs. They crave the others' appreciation, and love to receive compliments on themselves or their achievements. They have domineering personalities and prefer for things to happen fast. It's important to know that Reds, when hearing about personality colors, imagine themselves to be Yellow.

Reds are the greatest dandies among all the colors. They are vain and often narcissistic.

BLUES

Blues are easy to spot. They are born for adventure. They love traveling and noisy groups. Crave meeting new people and striking relationships. They know tons of people, but rarely remember how they'd met. They talk a lot, are very curious and often fail to listen. They have sharp wits and keep thinking about numerous things at once. Easy to distract and not fond of discipline. Convincing in their words, but faltering in their actions. Usually need someone to finish what they started. Very creative and outgoing people. Full of enthusiasm, and just like Reds, want for things to happen fast. They love money because it is a source of fun and pleasure.

It's a subtle distinction between Reds and Blues, but there are a few telltale traits to help tell them apart. Both Reds and Blues are show-offs and unconsciously enjoy other people's envy.

Discipline is a defining characteristic of Reds that Blues lack entirely. Blues are unable to garner self-discipline, it should be imposed on them from outside.

Unlike Blues, **Reds** are never late as they value punctuality an awful lot and don't enjoy working with people who are constantly late. When they are in charge of such people, Reds take great effort in reforming them.

Reds are on a mission to create copies of themselves, something totally outside Blues' aspirations, which are the exact opposite. Blues are confident in their own uniqueness and originality, and fervently believe none can be like them.

Blues more easily become the center of attention, they're more charismatic than Reds, because Reds are always careful not to stain their reputation. They behave

overbearingly and act with self-imposed seriousness, while Blues have no such qualms.

Blues can admire others, telling them how great and important they are, how smart and impressive. They know their own weaknesses and like being surrounded by skilled people, because they are well aware of how important those are for the achievement of their goals. And being excellent manipulators, it's not hard for them to be well-liked. Reds are not inclined to flattery. Their tremendous egos get in the way of such praise. They are capable of admiring only people who have achieved much in the past and are now gone, or people with great past accomplishments who have already fallen from favor and are now lower on the social ladder.

Reds are usually more hot-tempered and testy, allowing themselves to curse and raise their voice, while Blues are more diplomatic and sly. They don't achieve their goals by shouts and threats.

I don't want you to consider Reds bad people, just the opposite. Their business success is not coincidental. They are guardians and protectors of everything of their own. It's true they regard their employees as exclusive property and believe these people remain in their debt for life, but on the other hand, they are willing to protect them and care for them as if they were their own children.

If you admit your mistake to a Red and ask for guidance, they'll feel flattered, even though they won't show it. You'll probably be forgiven and provided with valuable advice, which is in your best interest to at least pretend to follow. Then, in time, you should thank them for it and for all their help. Thus, you'll become their favorite.

Don't worry if you have initial doubts; after spending longer time in the person's company, you'll be able to guess their predominant color.

GREENS

People of science – methodical, inquisitive, precise and analytical. Boring, humble, without a notable personality and charisma. Love to read and always depend on information from research and reliable sources. Never make emotional or rash decisions; before making up their mind, they must know everything and have all their questions answered. It takes them long to arrive at an important decision, but once the decision is made, hardly anything can prevent them from finishing what they started. They hate hugging, don't enjoy gatherings and parties. Avoid making new friends. Know everything in detail and can answer any questions. They love to show competence and thoroughness, but don't offer them wild parties, drunken nights and adventures full of adrenaline.

They're dependable and precise in everything they do, can take and handle responsibilities. For obvious reasons, Greens find team work difficult.

They are loyal friends and if you've made it to their friend list, it means you are special. They don't have many friends, but the ones they regard as such are people they trust and have let come closer. They are extremely protective of their privacy and very hard to win over.

They often become accountants, scientists, doctors, or architects, and if they set their minds to running a business, they're usually successful.

They are extremely patient and very consistent in their actions. Their penchant for analytics makes them scrutinize the state of their business often and then optimize it.

They are fond of trainings and extra qualifications. Enjoy talking to well-bred people and hate aggressive communication. They never permit themselves to call people names, but are adamant in their decisions.

Greens rarely, if ever, make impulsive decisions, unless it's about buying a bottle of water or a pack of gum. They are conservative, visit the same restaurants, but like change and always think it through. You cannot manipulate them with last copies left or huge bargains.

Greens rarely wear trendy clothes. Their appearance doesn't matter to them the way it matters to Reds.

YELLOWS

Gracious people who love to help others. They are not impressed by money, business success, or wealthy and luxurious lifestyles. Not interested in travels and adventures, although they enjoy hearing about them. Don't like decision-making because they fear their decision can offend or hurt smeone.

Everyone loves them, they are friendly and humane. Love hugging. Trusting and always willing to answer a cry for help by both friends and strangers.

Yellows don't want to be envied at any cost. They would give up buying something if they found out the purchase would hurt someone or sour their mood.

They regularly put other people's interests before their own.

They are often involved in charity. It's typical for them to take care of stray animals and volunteer for humanitarian causes.

They don't have a materialistic bone in their body.

Sometimes, upon looking back, they feel lost, seeing how much others have built, while they have nothing. But their constant generosity robs them of the opportunity to own and to build. They are the most loved and everybody likes them. Loyal friends, and although they don't always realize it, they are extremely rich, full of good intentions and detached from the material world. Unfortunately, often lonely and care-worn.

For the purposes of successful communication, in the following pages we'll examine a series of examples to help you remember personality colors and apply them in your work. In-depth knowledge of them will give you the opportunity to be more convincing both at your sales meetings and when motivating employees to fulfil a particular task.

But before you start working with people in this manner, it is imperative you determine your own predominant color.

I always include personality colors in my seminars on effective sales, and practice has shown me that a person rarely identifies their own color correctly, because from the way I've described them, nobody is perfect!

Reds stay silent and refuse to acknowledge the facts, Greens openly deny them; perhaps only Blues admit they are Blues. Out of modesty, Yellows paint themselves as Greens or Blues.

The truth is, we're an amalgam of colors; one is predominant, and the others complement it in the best possible way. We're all awesome and wonderful. But to determine your predominant color, you may ask someone who knows you well to read this chapter and try to classify you. I think they may do a better job than if you tried on your own.

And you, Reds, I know you are good people, but please don't fool yourselves, you're not Yellow. ☺

AN EXAMPLE OF MOTIVATING DIFFERENT PERSONALITY TYPES

You are **Mr. Dikov**, the CEO of a large sales company which has offices all over the country. You want marketing director Boris and his assistant Stoil to do a series of trainings with the sales teams, but both of them have to be motivated and approach the task with interest and eagerness, because the trainings must be highly effective.

Boris, as the one in charge, will be Blue, Green, Red or Yellow in the different scenarios. Stoil will have the personality color most suitable for the fulfilment of the task.

SCENARIO I (a): Director Boris is Blue, which means his assistant Stoil better be Yellow. You are Mr. Dikov.

Conversation between Mr. Dikov and Boris:

"Hello, Boris. I have the job just for you." (Evoking curiosity.)

"Really? What is it?"

"It's not work, exactly, more of a pleasant assignment that involves traveling across the country. I'm sure nobody can do it better, because you are the best at communication. It will be real fun. Are you listening?" (This question encourages Boris to focus when you are about to announce the essence of the job.)

"Sure!"

"You'll have to visit all our offices around the country and hold regional training sessions. It will also be an opportunity to meet all our sales reps, and you'll spend every day at a different place. On the whole, I believe it will be very interesting."

"Great, when do I leave?"

"Well, first we must have *you* trained, so that you can pass it to the others."

"Sure, when does the training start? I can't wait to be gone!"

"Soon, but there's one more thing, please listen carefully. (Again focusing his attention.) After your training session, all employees will sit an exam, and if a large number don't pass, you'll be held responsible. (Blues often doubt their success, so this is a great opportunity to involve another in the assignment. Thus, the responsibility will be shared, and if needed, shifted on the other.) That's why I think it best for Stoil to come with you. In this way, you'll not be bored on the road (Blues don't like to be bored even for a minute), and you'll also be able to count on Stoil – you know he's always ready to help."

"Yes, I think we should start the training immediately. You can assign anyone for my assistant, I don't mind. I can manage on my own, but it really will be better to have someone to talk to in the car. I also think–" (Here you should interrupt if you want to ever finish this conversation.)

"All right, Bobby. Tomorrow I'll set the date for your training, and after passing your exam, you'll become an instructor and go to train the others."

"Okay, I think the training better start tomorrow, we needn't waste time."

"Bye, Bobby!"

Now we have to motivate Stoil, who is Yellow.

"Hi, Stoil, smiling and positive, as always."

"Thank you, Mr. Dikov."

"See, I set Boris a task, but you know how he is, always talking and rarely listening to what he is told. I'm worried whether he will be up to the task."

"Is there anything I can do?"

"Yes, I think you can be of great help. We have to hold regional sales training sessions all around the country.

Will you help Boris and me with this difficult and essential task?"

"Of course, Mr. Dikov. I'm so excited you chose me to help. I'll do my best to make everything go smoothly."

"Thank you a lot, Stoil. You have to go through the training yourself, then you and Boris leave for the country. If you can, please help Boris prepare, he'll hardly manage it without you. And you know, this conversation should stay between us – we don't want to ruin Boris's self-esteem. Better no one knows that your mission is to help and prevent possible disaster; we don't want anyone to take offence." (Yellows would never wish to hurt, offend or annoy anyone.)

"Yes, you know you can count on me. Let me hug you."

Now you can rest assured you have motivated both your employees for the task, and they will be happy to do it!

In this case, you shouldn't send a Blue Stoil with Boris, because they'll turn the job into an endless celebration. They'll be both too busy talking and won't hear a single question from their trainees. There'll be parties every night, and trouble waking up in the morning. The possibility of the training being highly ineffective is pretty great.

You also cannot send a Green Stoil, unless you'd like to ship him to a psychiatric ward right after or lose him forever as a valuable asset. He won't be able to withstand Boris's constant chatter, will get stressed from meeting so many new people, and traveling will tire him greatly. And you don't want him preparing for the training for months until he feels completely ready to face this challenge.

Neither can you send a Red Stoil to assist Boris, because it will be a torture for him. In such a situation, Stoil would like to play the main part and be the leading coach, and have Boris as his assistant.

To have such an unreliable person like Boris in charge? Impossible. And even if Stoil feels obliged to accept the job, the two will be at their throats as soon as they hit the road, and you don't want arguments and conflict between them.

SCENARIO I (b): Director Boris is Red, which means his assistant Stoil better be Yellow or Green.

Conversation between Mr. Dikov and Boris:

"Hello, Boris. Looking good, like always." (Reds adore compliments.)

"Thanks, boss. You seem to be in top shape, too."
"I have a job for you."

"Sure, just say the word and consider it done."

"We need to hold regional sales training sessions around the country, and I know no one can handle it better than you."

"Thanks for trusting me, boss. I'm glad we're on the same page."

"To do the trainings, you have to be trained yourself and pass an exam. I believe it won't be a problem for you."

"I wouldn't worry if I were you. You know it'll be a slam dunk."

"I know, that's why I'm assigning it to you. Nobody can better organize and manage people."

"You flatter me, Mr. Dikov."

"I don't want you wasting your talent on trivia, so I'm sending Stoil along."

"But boss, that won't be necessary, I can manage the job fine on my own."

"I know, but I don't want you wasting time with minor details. That's what Stoil's for. He'll take care of the odds and ends, and you'll focus on the more serious and essential part of the job."

"Okay. Stoil's a good guy, I like him." (Who doesn't like Yellows, and they pose no threat to an ambitious Red.)

"He is. After passing the exam, I'll assign the two of you your tasks, and you start training the rest."

"Better give all the tasks to me, then I'll assign Stoil the ones I consider appropriate."

"I don't doubt you, Boris, but let me assign the tasks. I wouldn't want you giving Stoil an errand he can't handle."

"Okay, then that's what we'll do." (If a Red hasn't made the decision himself, it should be a mutual decision, or you risk making him feel awkward. But you want him motivated, so you'd better be diplomatic.)

Now we have to motivate Stoil, who is Yellow.

"Hi Stoil. Smiling and positive, like always."

"Thank you, Mr. Dikov."

"See, I set Boris a task, but you know how impulsive he is. I'm worried there may be trouble in one of the offices."

"Is there anything I can do?"

"Yes, I think you can be of great help. We have to hold regional sales training sessions all around the country. Will you help Boris and me with this difficult and essential task?"

"Of course, Mr. Dikov. I'm so excited you chose me to help. I'll do my best to make everything go smoothly."

"Thank you a lot, Stoil. You have to go through the training yourself, then you and Boris leave for the country. And you know, this conversation should stay between us – we don't want to ruin Boris's self-esteem. Better no one knows that your mission is to help and prevent possible disaster; we don't want him to take offence." (Yellows would never wish to hurt, offend or annoy anyone.)

"Yes, you know you can count on me. Let me hug you."

Now you can rest assured you have motivated your employees for the task, and they will be happy to do it.

You cannot send a Red Stoil to assist Boris, who is also Red, because that would mean war. In such circumstances, Stoil will want to play the main part and have Boris as his assistant.

They are both capable and diligent, but they won't be able to share the limelight. Even if Stoil feels obliged to accept, during the trip there will be arguments and conflict, which will negatively affect the training. They will be constantly pitting themselves against each other.

You also shouldn't send a Blue Stoil along with Boris, because he'll fill Boris's head with twaddle and annoy him even before they arrive, which may have an undesirable effect on the trainings. Stoil would like to have fun, he'll distract the trainees with jokes and funny stories, while Boris would expect the job to be handled seriously and attentively. He won't pass the opportunity of repeatedly criticizing Stoil, which may cause tension and even conflict between them.

You may send a Green Stoil, although you'll be risking him getting rather stressed from the situation and all that travel.

On the whole, it won't be a very pleasant experience for him, but you can easily motivate him: he'll appreciate Boris's leadership skills, and even if he notices omissions in the trainings, he won't criticize openly, because such people try to avoid trouble. On the other hand, Stoil will be very useful for the trainings themselves, because he will be able to provide competent answers to all questions, and he'll analyze and asses the trainees.

Here's how to motivate Green Stoil to help Red Boris:

"Hi Stoil, lost in thought as ever, huh?"

"Yes, Mr. Dikov, I was thinking."

"See, I need your advice."

"Sure. What's the problem, Mr. Dikov?"

"I set Boris the task to hold regional sales trainings in all our offices around the country. But that's not an easy assignment for a single person, what do you think?"

"He's energetic, Mr. Dikov, and you know he'll be eager to prove himself, but maybe you really should send an assistant."

"Yes, I was wondering whether you are up for the job. It will be useful to have you with him, you can take notes during the trainings. And I know you are always ready to answer questions. Your work is detailed and precise, and I cannot think of a better person for the job."

"I don't know, I'll have to think about it."

"Sure, that's a serious assignment and I don't expect you to decide right away. Think it through for a few days. But I'd like to know whether you accept this challenging task by the end of the week." (Never rush Greens for an answer unless you'd like to be refused. But you also shouldn't give them too long to deliberate, because you risk them being at it for months.)

"Okay, I'll think about it. Is there any information on the trainings I could look through?" (Greens not asking for information, impossible.)

"Yes, I'll give you the syllabus, but I'm sure it will be easy as pie for you."

End of the week.

"Hello Stoil, did you make up your mind?"

"Would it be too late to answer on Monday, Mr. Dikov? Thus, I'll have time to ponder it more carefully over the weekend."

"Sure, tomorrow or Monday, it's all the same to me. But on Monday I want your answer."

Monday.

"Hi Stoil, did you decide yet?"

"To be honest, I'm not sure. Traveling worries me a little, I don't know."

"You think you couldn't handle the task?"

"No, the training itself is a piece of cake. Over the weekend, I read carefully through all the questions. I could probably pass the exam even without attending the course, but I'm not sure."

"Don't you think it will be interesting? You can sit in the back and observe the training, taking notes, answering questions. I'll count on you for analysis and conclusions afterwards."

"Okay, I'll help Boris. I can do it."

"Of course you can. Who could do it better than you?"

"I don't know, but I can do it. I accept the challenge." (For Greens, everything outside their usual routine is a challenge, even going to a night club.)

"Okay, but I'd rather nobody knew about our conversation. You know how arrogant Boris can be."

"Sure, I don't want any intrigue. Everyone has their job to do."

"Thank you for understanding, Stoil."

"I thank you for your trust, Mr. Dikov."

SCENARIO I (c): Manager Boris is Green, which means Stoil better be Yellow or Green like Boris.

In such a scenario, you cannot send a Red Stoil, because we know Reds are leaders and like to run the show. And since you don't want to cause conflict, you won't send a Red to assist Boris. You also cannot send a Blue. We already know Blues and Greens don't work in harmony and agreement. They are too different to be a proper team.

If you decide to send two Greens, it would mean a very serious preparation before they accept the task. You can also be sure that the time assigned for the trainings will never be enough – they are thorough and descriptive, so they'll want the trainees to have everything explained in detail. But, on the other hand, they'll hold wonderful sessions, and we'll get analyses and recommendations for our next trainings. They'll also provide plenty of information about our reps in different regions and their level of competence. In short, we can always count on Greens. And be sure that their audience won't ask for new trainings for at least a year. They are not particularly funny, and their slow talking and descriptive approach to the subject will lose the attention of all Blue and Red colleagues.

Things look rather similar if Boris is Green and Stoil – Yellow.

You already know Yellows love to help, it doesn't matter to them whether they will be heads or assistants. The trainings will go smoothly and last quite long. I believe you can also guess how to motivate them.

You can use the examples above to encourage Boris and Stoil to accept the task if they are both Green, or if Boris is Green and Stoil is Yellow.

SCENARIO I (d): Manager Boris is Yellow, which means Stoil better be Green or Yellow like Boris, but he could also be Blue.

In this scenario, it won't do for Stoil to be Red because, as you already know, Reds like to lead. So Stoil will feel down, and although he likes Boris as a person, he won't feel comfortable as his assistant. It's unlikely for conflicts to arise because Yellows are always ready to yield, but if you have a choice, you'd better not put Red Stoil's will and patience to the test.

If you send Yellow Stoil to assist Yellow Boris, the trainings will go smoothly and involve a lot of hugging. A friendly atmosphere will prevail in all the offices.

If you ask about the sales reps' competences, you'd be told they are all great and very capable. There's a good chance for the reps in the regional offices to get a little help with the tests by their instructors, or happen to see the correct answers from filled up sheets left "accidentally" on a desk.

You can rely on Yellows to do the trainings, but the results may not be quite accurate.

If you send a Green Stoil along with Boris, that will be a good solution. Thus, the trainings will pass more slowly, but be more effective. Nobody will be able to cheat at the exam because Stoil won't allow it – unless Boris helps his colleagues while Stoil is out for a smoke or has his attention on a curious reading material someone "accidentally" left close by.

The two will be a good and slightly boring team, but you can trust them.

You can also send a Blue Stoil to assist Yellow Boris. Then, besides really friendly trainings, we risk the Blues in the group sniffing one another out and holding regular parties leading to late mornings. As you know,

Yellows cannot say "no", so they'll both be at the parties. There will be harmony and Boris will never demonstrate superiority over Stoil. But you won't get any analysis or reliable information on the reps' competence.

As I already mentioned, Yellows are slightly naïve, and a Blue will easily convince a Yellow to go for a drink, which will turn out to be several drinks, and there's no guarantee at what time the next morning's session will start.

Don't worry; if such a thing occurs, unlike the Blue, the Yellow will admit to everything.

Having said all that, even if it was humorous and slightly exaggerated, let's see what conclusions we can draw.

Everyone could be assigned the job, but to make a good team, we have to pick both people carefully, and set their respective tasks even more carefully.

It's better for business to motivate people separately, because factors that stimulate one can put off another.

Managers often send people to hold training sessions depending on their positions within the company, without taking their personalities into account. This is considered a huge mistake.

But in order to cleverly use people's personality colors in effective sales and persuasive communication, you must learn to recognize them as fast as possible.

HOW TO IDENTIFY A PERSON'S COLOR?

If you've known someone for a long time, I'm sure you already know their color. But if you have met recently or are about to meet for the first time, you'd better learn to ask the right questions that will help you recognize the color.

Ask what the person does for a living. Although some people's jobs do not match their color, in most cases the answer to this question will point you in the right direction.

If they are involved in science, physics, research, accounting or architecture, they are probably Green.

Take notice what they enjoy doing in their free time. If they have none, insisting that time is money or that they are too busy with their business, they are probably Red or Blue.

If they spend their free time caring about stray animals, helping the poor or engaged in charity, they are Yellow.

If however, they have lots of time on their hands and cannot say what exactly they keep spending it on, their predominant color is probably Blue. If they are constantly reading or working on new inventions, they are most likely Green.

You may think of many more guiding questions to help you identify the color, but don't turn your conversation into an interrogation. Put in questions only when appropriate and don't focus all your attention on this task. In time, you'll realize it's not difficult to sense a person's predominant color even in an ordinary conversation.

HOW TO GRAB THE ATTENTION OF DIFFERENT COLORS?

When you want to capture a Red's attention, talk to them about money and power, business and its brilliant prospects, about the opportunity to manage and control lots of people. Pay the Red person a compliment – or two, or three, and they'll like you and support you. If you want to make them do something, just challenge them. Express doubts in their abilities or simply mention that another could do the job better, and just watch. Of course, by repeating these actions, you may push their buttons as many times as you'd like, and restart them again and again. When you want to draw a Blue's attention, mention entertainment, travel and meeting new people, also partying till dawn, but don't underestimate the appeal of money. They are quite the materialistic money lovers. And yet, if you want them to do something for you, don't call it work. They don't enjoy working, except when it involves a world trip or another fun, entertaining activity.

Yellows can be won by talking about social causes – helping the homeless, poor, sick or orphaned. They will embark enthusiastically on the job, ready to respond to every cry for help. But don't abuse their kindness, because if a Yellow removes you from his friend list, you'll be forever denied access to their heart. Greens are charmed by websites, books and other information sources. Pique their curiosity and don't put a time limit – let them do the research, and at the end, they'll be sold all by themselves. They are useful, analytical and productive.

STIMULATING THOUGHTS AND EXPRESSIONS

To master persuasive communication, besides knowing people's colors, you should be skillful at using different stimulating thoughts and expressions which will spur them into doing the task you have in mind.

Let's say you're considering a startup and looking for employees and partners. You want them to be more motivated than ever to work on your project. You should use the business's advantages and strong points to provoke people and arouse their interest. And of course, you should announce you intentions the right way, using stimulating expressions.

Example I: You share your business idea with Itso, who is Green and works as system administrator.

"Hi Itso."

"Hi Joro."

"You know, there are two kinds of people. Those who drive to work and spend three hours in traffic every day, and those who work from home?"

"Yes, and I belong to the first group, unfortunately."

"But everyone knows the second group is better off."

"Sure, I know it too, but I still can't garner enough courage to strike out on my own."

"I have both bad and good news for you. Which do you want first?"

"Start with the bad, then."

"Okay. Come Monday, you're out of a job."

"What are you talking about, who told you that?"

"Easy, I'm telling it to you, because the good news is, I have another job for you that will make you one of those people working from home."

"You do? What job?"

"You'll take care of the company website of my new enterprise, and you won't need to come to the office."

"Sounds great, what's the money?"

"In the beginning, until we develop the business, it won't be very much, but then it'll grow. Which would be easier for you, working from home for less money at first, or being one of those nuts traveling half a day to the office?"

"You're right, it's a burden. I get so tired and stressed out. But still, money matters."

"Of course it does. If you'd rather pass, I know who else to ask. I just wanted to try you first, seeing you're such a close friend."

By claiming that there are two kinds of people, you impress on Itso that he's among the unlucky ones. Everyone knows it's better to belong to the second group. The good and bad news trick is used to highlight the advantages. The bad news startles Itso, so he sees the good as a way out.

Thus, you've made him welcome your good news, although the bad was not actually true. It's up to him whether he'll quit or not. But in other circumstances, he may not pay enough attention to your proposal, because he's too conservative, so by structuring the conversation in this way, you make him consider it.

Even if he doesn't accept right away, the question "Which would be easier for you?" will probably make him look for the easier way. And by assuring him that you have other people in mind for the position, you make it clear you don't want to pressure him, it's just an offer. Greens shouldn't be hassled because they would just say no.

Example II: You share your business idea with Peppy, who is Red and works as sales manager in a small trading company.

"Hello Peppy."

"Hi Joro."

"You know, most people turn down great opportunities without even batting an eye."

"Indeed, people are such fools. I'm constantly having to deal with such."

"There's an old saying that wealthy people have never missed an opportunity."

"Sure, there's always truth to those old sayings, Jorka."

"See, most people want to start their own business so they are free and financially independent."

"Yeah, I wish I were independent too, and one day I will be. I'm sure this day is coming."

"Peppy, some people keep wishing and never lift a finger, while others work to achieve their goals. Which group do you belong to?"

"Definitely the second one."

"I'm just about to launch a new business and I'm looking for partners. True, it will be hard at first, but private business is a great way to achieve financial independence."

"I don't know, Joro. It probably won't make much money at first, and I have lots of expenses. And I'll have to invest in it, won't I?"

"Sure, you will. But it's up to you, and you know better: which will be easier for you? "Firing" your boss and working for financial freedom, or allowing him to burden you with responsibilities every day for a fixed salary, and tomorrow, when you're no longer needed, to show you the door? You're well aware how much he benefits from you."

"Ha-ha, firing your boss, I like that. Still, you need to tell me more about this project."

"Sure, Peppy, I will. There are two kinds of people: winners like you and me, and everybody else."

"We'll show them, Joro! Let's get to work, the boss can sort out his own messes."

By telling Peppy most people turn down opportunities without thinking, you're paving the way. Then you share your business idea, presenting it as an excellent opportunity he shouldn't pass by. The old saying about wealthy people never missing an opportunity is your next hook. Most people believe that as long as something is an "old saying", it must be true. But of course, you give Peppy the option of backing away, asking him which would be easier for him. You can hardly expect him to prefer working for a mere salary; after all, he's Red.

By dividing people into those who achieve their goals and those who don't, as well as into winners and everybody else, we conclude our persuasive communication. Now Peppy will be motivated to win and will work hard to accomplish his goals and prove his competence. Don't forget, that's among the Reds' fortes. Once they set themselves a goal, they pursue it single-mindedly.

Example III: You share your business idea with Krassy, who is Yellow and works as a storeroom supervisor in a pharmaceutical company, and volunteers in a charity organization in his free time.

"Krassy, hello."

"Hi Joro."

"Everybody knows that true friends support each other, right?"

"Sure, that's what friends are for!"

"I'm curious, would you support a business who sets aside part of its profits for charity?"

"Of course, you know charity's exactly what I do in my spare time."

"You know Krassy, there're two kinds of people – good and kind like you, and everybody else."

"Thanks Jorka, there are also many people who need help."

"Yes, I know. That's why I want to invite you to participate in my new project. At first, it will be difficult and I don't know how much we are going to earn. But when business starts going strong, we'll all benefit. Then we can set aside a percentage of our profit to help people in need."

"That will be great! If it pans out, I would be able to build a children's home, or maybe an animal shelter."

"Sure, Krassy. Most people would pursue their dreams. That's what the two of us we'll do, right?"

"Yes, Joro, just tell me what you want from me, and let's do it."

Example IV: You share your business idea with Ivo, who is Blue and works as a dreamer.

"Hello Ivo."

"Hi Joro."

"You know, most people want to have their own business so that they have money and time to travel and enjoy life."

"Really? Then I'd like to have one, too."

"Ivo, there are two kinds of people: dreamers and pragmatics. Which group do you belong to?"

"I don't know, I'm a dreamer, I guess. I dream of traveling the world once by plane, and then once more by ship."

"Have you heard that wise tale about the dreamer who passed away without fulfilling none of their dreams?"

"Actually, no. It sounds awful, can you tell me more of it?"

"I don't remember it well either, because I'm a pragmatic, I just remembered this bit. Bu tell me, which will be easier for you, Ivo: leaving your dreams stay dreams, or doing something to make them come true?"

"Well, I want to, but I don't know what to do."

"Old people say, there's always a way out and good opportunities ahead. We just shouldn't pass them by."

"Yeah, old people are usually wise."

"You know, I'm starting a new business and I'd want you to participate. It will be fun, and if things go well, we'll all benefit. And you'll have enough money to travel the world and have fun."

"Sounds great, I'll be happy to join."

"Don't you want me to tell you what it's about first?"

"Doesn't matter, I'll do anything you say if it helps me fulfil my dreams."

"Okay, here's what I want from you."

Blues are easy to identify and even easier to convince. Just tell them there will be traveling, parties and fun, and they are on board. But don't harbor great expectations about what they will actually do. They burn out just as easily as they flare up. You need to keep them motivated at all times, or you risk them losing interest in the idea pretty quickly.

Remember, people prefer the conversation to be revolving around them – to understand what's in it for them, depending on their particular needs. Besides, people enjoy being told stories and sayings. They like to have a choice when they are faced with a decision.

A large number of them like to do the same as "most people". Our brains function in such a way that, if we believe everybody knows something, that means we know it too, so it must be true. As long as it is a saying or an old adage, it's wise and must be good advice.

And if there are two kinds of people, we definitely must belong to the cooler group!

That's why it's handy to use expressions like "there are two kinds of people", "I have good news and bad news", "there's an old saying that goes …", "everybody knows that", "most people so and so", "which will be easier for you", "let me tell you a story". They'll help you to be more convincing, to provoke your opponent's interest and achieve your goals.

You should only be more careful when talking to Greens, because it's highly likely that you drew blank. They don't like empty chatter, and the fact that they listen in silence doesn't mean they believe you. If they sense you are trying to manipulate them, they'll immediately lose interest in you and your story.

Regardless of whether you are involved in distance or direct sales, don't ever try to apply one strategy to all. That will lead to much less satisfying results.

THE CHAMELEON

Andrey cut quite the dashing figure with his slender frame, broad shoulders, high cheekbones and charming smile. His mind was cutthroat sharp, he was a pleasant

companion, always ready with a witty comeback and a quick smile. He chatted with everybody, was always quick to lend a hand, and was quite good at his job. He was a business consultant in a huge consulting agency, and his clients enjoyed dealing with him and often asked for his services. His results were more than satisfactory.

Andrey was interesting and clever, very skilled at maneuvering, and managed to get himself liked by all, especially the ladies. His reputation of a Don Juan was well earned; women noticed him and used every opportunity to flirt with him. But there was one lovely lady who paid him no mind: Bogdana, humble and astoundingly beautiful. This lady, whose name meant "gift from God", worked as a chief accountant and accounting consultant in the agency. Despite her simple and modest clothes, she had the air of a goddess. Tall and slim, with chestnut hair and large hazel eyes, she always smelled of a subtle perfume which suited her very well. She rarely smiled, but when she did, all guys in the office wished they were gone so that they wouldn't endure the torture of not being with her. Although she could have picked anyone, she was still single. She went to lunch with her female coworkers, and after work, she refused all the men's polite invitations to drive her home, and took the subway by herself. Andrey fancied her too, but he knew he had no chance of capturing her heart, especially given his reputation.

One day, a client came to the agency looking for an accounting consultant. Andrey invited the man in the visitors' lounge and kept him company while they waited for an available consultant. Andrey told a curious story, and just as they were laughing at its funny ending, Bogdana entered. Both their smiles instantly froze, and the visitor stared in awe.

"Hello sir, sorry to keep you waiting. But I see my colleague here helped you pass away the time. Pleased to meet you, I'm Bogdana."

"Hello. I don't know who I am. The moment I saw you, I forgot my name and the reason I'm here."

Bogdana ignored the man's attempt at wittiness. "Well, since I'm the chief accountant, I assume you need accounting or financial advice."

"Indeed, but now I think I also need an aspirin."

Andrey laughed at the visitor's new attempt to win the young woman's favor, but Bogdana only sighed and asked, "Would you like a glass of water?"

"No, madam, they offered me already, thank you. It was just a joke. I hope I haven't made you feel awkward with my cheesy lines."

"No problem. Can we please get to the point now?"

"Yes, absolutely. I left a suitcase with all the accounting papers of one of my companies with the assistant here. I want you to examine them and tell me if you notice anything amiss. I suspect my accountants of diverting funds, but I cannot be sure. Please call me anytime if you need further information. I'm up to speed with the business but I cannot monitor all the expenses. And my knowledge of accounting is too limited to uncover a potential problem by myself."

"Okay, we can take your case right away. How much time do we have?"

"I was hoping you could check it all in about a month. What do you say?"

"It's too much time. We'll get back to you in two weeks."

"Great, how much do I owe you?"

"You can discuss fees with Andrey. I'll see to it that the job is done expertly and on time. But I still don't know you name, Mr...?"

"Gavril Ivanov. Although my friends call me Chameleon."

"Alright, Mr. Ivanov, we'll be in touch as soon as we have news."

"Thank you, madam. You were very kind."

Bogdana went out, leaving the men to reach an agreement and sign a contract.

"Andrey, please prepare all the papers and send them to my email. I'm not in the mood for dealing with contracts right now."

"No problem, Mr. Ivanov. You said they called you Chameleon. Do you mind telling me where this nickname comes from?"

"No, it's fine. Over the years, I learned to recognize different personality types, and the more I perfected this skill, the more successful my business became. My friends started seeing me as a chameleon who adapts to every environment, every conversation, every personality. So they began calling me so."

"That's fascinating. I hope I'm not pestering you with my questions."

"It's okay. You know, Andrew, your colleague is an extraordinary girl."

"I know. Everybody is attracted to her, but she's a little weird. To be honest, I'm quite popular with the ladies, but with her, I stand no chance. She's really distanced, and it feels like she spurns all worldly pleasures."

"I don't think so. If you ask me, she's just waiting for her Prince Charming. Something made her lose faith in men. Perhaps someone hurt her or something. I believe I can help you win her heart."

"Really?"

"Yeah. Tell me what you know about her and her family."

"Not much. I've heard her mother is a research scholar, but I know nothing of her father. She always has her nose buried in a book. The girls she has lunch with say she's a very capable accountant despite being so young. She doesn't enjoy eating out, I think she's not much into partying either. A girl from the office said she visited Bogdana at home and was fascinated by her place. It was really neat and tidy, and one entire room was converted into a library."

"Does she have a hobby?"

"Yes, they say she likes dabbling in fashion design. She has dozens of designs done just for fun. Which surprises me, given the way she dresses."

"Does she have a pet?"

"Yes, a cat. I know nothing more, I haven't seen it."

"Doesn't she post pictures online?"

"Are you kidding? Her Facebook profile is restricted. Most of her friends have no access to any information, me included. Perhaps her female friends have, I haven't thought to check. Why do you ask?"

"Andrey, this woman is very beautiful and very private. That's why you've all gone crazy about her. To win her, you have to do your research and then play an intelligent game. Would you have lunch with me? I'll tell you more about personality types, and together, we can come up with a strategy for capturing her heart."

"It will be my pleasure, Mr. Ivanov."

"Please call me Gavril, no need to be so formal."

"Okay, Gavril, there's a restaurant close by."

"Let me take you to one of my favorite places. They always have a table ready for me. Somewhere we can talk."

"Sure, let's go."

Andrey was quite excited at meeting the Chameleon. This successful businessman, not even a friend of his, already offered to help and teach him invaluable lessons about people. Moreover, he was ready to help him win Bogdana. Andrey had no idea why a stranger would do so much for him, but he was happy with the way things were going. Only half an hour later, they were in a lovely restaurant, seated at a table with a magnificent view, surrounded by greenery and flowers.

"Why are you doing all this for me, Gavril?"

"Truth is, you remind me of myself twenty years ago. Strong-willed, charming, energetic, passionate. One day, I met a man who helped me greatly to understand people, and taught me how to be a strategist and a winner. Now I'm teaching you, and one day, you'll pay it forward to some other lucky guy."

"Thank you, Gavril."

Gavril went on explaining about personality colors and ways to motivate people. He stressed the importance of being a strategist and working for your reputation. And finally, the moment came to tell Andrey how to capture Bogdana's interest. "What does she know about you?"

"Not much. She must presume I'm an awful flirt."

"Okay, so it's time to bust this myth and show her you're her prince."

"And how can I do this?"

"Let's piece her profile together first. Do you know her zodiacal sign?"

"Yes, Virgo."

"Great, so we know she loves her family and puts them first. She's not fond of parties and clubs, but she loves animals, or at least cats. Her hobby is fashion design. Also, she's an experienced, hard-working accountant. Bogdana doesn't seek new friendships and is very protective of her privacy. She's Green and perhaps a bit Yellow."

"Yes, I guess she is. And I think I'm Yellow, too."

"No, pal, you're Red. Reds often fancy themselves Yellow."

"You really think I'm Red?"

"I do, and perhaps a little Blue."

"Yeah, maybe you're right. But let's get back to Bogdana."

"Bogdana probably expects the man of her dreams to be handsome and athletic like her – you fit the bill nicely. This man should also be humble and dedicated to science, or at least have a serious profession. Moreover, he'd better be successful, or at least reliable, with a bright future ahead of him. Bogdana's dream guy must love animals, especially cats, and be polite and gallant to people. He shouldn't be too pushy and press her into making decisions. She wouldn't fall for a flirt or a person enjoying nightclubs and bars. Just the opposite: she's looking for a man who loves children and cares for his family. Bogdana would like this man to take care of her; although she's independent, she'd like to rely on her partner's protection. If you decide to pursue her, I'm afraid you'll have to make lots of concessions."

"Wow, as if she were a book you read through in an instant."

"Most people are like this, open books. Tell me, now, Andrey, what's my color?"

"Yellow, I guess?"

"No, Andrey, I'm the Chameleon! A combination of all the colors. I switch colors to achieve my goals. Originally, I was a lot like you, but I changed in the last twenty years."

"Right, the Chameleon. So what do you suggest I do to win over Bogdana?"

"You really still want to do that?"

"I do. And have her forever."

"Gosh, forever. Are you telling me you want to marry her?"

"Maybe it sounds weird, but she's the girl of my dreams."

"Okay then, let's come up with a strategy."

"Right."

The conversation lasted for a long time. They discussed Bogdana and her views of life. And after a few hours of talking, they had their strategy. Now Andrey had to sign for an accountancy course and at some point, ask Bogdana to help him study for his exam. He had to adopt a cat and play the role of a man determined to change his life in pursuit of his dreams, which he would share with Bogdana while she helped him with his lessons. His dreams, of course, were of a loving family, a stable and well-paid job, a beautiful and smart wife with whom to grow old happy. Having lots of kids was not yet on the table because he didn't know Bogdana's opinion on large families. He also had to buy more books and read all Bogdana's favorites. Of course, he had to learn more about her, but not by asking her close friends. So one of the first steps in his strategy was to create a female Facebook profile and seek Bogdana's friendship.

"Thank you, Gavril, I believe meeting you is going to change my life. Can I call you if I need advice?"

"Sure you can. And don't forget to send me the contract for your company's services."

"I won't, and you'll get the best prices."

Gavril smiled, paid the bill and the two friends left the restaurant. Andrey couldn't wait to pursue his goal, following Gavril's brilliant strategy. This very night he found some pictures of a female friend of his who had recently moved to Canada, and created a fake Facebook profile. He decided to call his alter ego Jasmina, a Bulgarian accountant who was now living in Canada. He put up the few pictures he had, and sent a friendship request to one of Bogdana's friends. A week later, three of them were already on his friend list. Andrey had enrolled on an accountancy and control course, and because he knew their office assistant was close to Bogdana, he started ordering accountancy books and resources, to be delivered at the office. When the assistant handed them to him, she asked why Andrey needed all of this. That was exactly what he wanted; he knew the assistant will tell everyone about his new pursuit, and it would inevitably reach Bogdana, too.

In time, Jasmina – Andrey's fictitious female alter ego, managed to get among Bogdana's Facebook friends. And after a few more days of chatting, she was moved to the close friends list and now had access to all of

Bogdana's information. So now Andrey knew which her favorite books and movies were and saw pictures of her beloved cat, as well as some of her fashion designs.

One woman to another, Jasmina learned a lot about Bogdana; information she wouldn't have shared with any man. So Andrey was now reading several novels simultaneously, as well as watching the movies Bogdana had marked as favorite. He also adopted a kitten – a small miracle that brought a lot of good cheer to his empty apartment. From time to time, Andrey called Gavril to tell him how things were going. Gavril was also excited and curious whether the young man would be able to win his lady's affection by following his advice. Bogdana had called and met with Gavril, to tell him about the accounting discrepancies she had uncovered. She had pinpointed the problem, and it turned out Gavril's suspicions were well grounded. It seemed the man really knew people well.

One day, Andrey came across Bogdana in the office kitchen. He went for a cup of coffee, and she was just finishing a juicy red apple. "Hi Bogdana, I'm making myself coffee, would you like some?"

"Hi, Andrey. No, thanks, I already had one today. I heard you were getting into accounting – it was quite a surprise."

"Yeah, I've enrolled on a course, but I'm no good. I have an exam coming soon and I doubt that I'll be able to pass."

"Perhaps between women and bars you have no time left to study?"

"What made you say that? I hardly ever go out, and in the last month, not at all. And I don't know who's behind that stupid gossip about women. I don't even have a girlfriend, and most women nowadays are rather… Never mind, I don't want to offend anyone."

"Rather what?"

"Well, rather money-driven and easy, and that's not what I'm looking for. Anyway, I got to go, I have much work to do."

"Sure, bye."

Then Bogdana started mulling over their conversation. She liked Andrey, but she'd never told anybody. She knew about his frivolous attitude to women, but it was indeed an opinion formed by the office gossip. In fact, she had never seen him with a woman, nor had any female ever called him at the office. And coming to think about it, he was the only one in the building who had never hit on her. Did he not find her attractive?

Of course, the truth was entirely different. Andrey was sure Bogdana wouldn't agree to go out with him, so he had never bothered to ask her. He was born to win, and until now, he didn't believe he had a chance with her, so he ignored Bogdana despite considering her a great catch.

The next morning, he left one of her favorite books on the table in the visitors' lounge. He had seen that Bogdana had a scheduled meeting with a client, and hoped she would be curious who the book belonged to. Of course, he had taken the copy from the library so that it would look used and read more than once.

Bogdana's meeting ended, and she hurried to bring the book to the office assistant and ask if she knew who it belonged to. Her friend, who usually knew everything, now couldn't satisfy Bogdana's curiosity. Later in the afternoon,

Andrey shared with the assistant that he'd left his book in the visitors' lounge the previous night, and she handed it back to him in surprise, taking it out of the cupboard by her desk. Andrey grinned, took the book and went back to his office; all that was left now was for the assistant to tell Bogdana the book was his. It happened the very same day. Things were going exactly as planned.

The next day, Andrey again caught Bogdana alone in the kitchen. It was a great time to ask her for a favor, because they were alone and she was at ease. "Hi Bogdana, how's it going?"

"Fine, what about you?"

"I'm fine, thanks. But I'd like to ask for a favor. I don't want to bother you, but my accounting exam is getting near, and I'd really appreciate a little help. I'm sure you are very busy, so it's all right to say no."

"Don't worry, I'll help you. What's bothering you exactly?"

"There are a few things I can't wrap my head around. Perhaps we can go somewhere after work, and I'll show you?"

"Sure, no problem."

"Great, thanks. See you later then."

"Yeah. See you."

After work, Andrey showed Bogdana the things he failed to understand, and she plunged into a lengthy explanation. As usual, she exuded sweet charm, mixed with meekness. She looked hot and elegant even without wearing expensive clothes.

When she got carried away in her explanations, Andrey cut her short. "Sorry to interrupt, it's been really useful. But it's getting late and I have to go, I don't want my little sweetie to starve."

"Oh sure, no problem. Let's go, I have a lot to do at home, too. Is your … sweetheart much younger than you?" Slightly jealous and annoyed, Bogdana asked the very question Andrey had hoped for.

He laughed. "Yeah, quite younger actually, about 28 years, I guess."

"28 years?! Aren't you 28?"

"Exactly. My sweetie is this little helpless stray kitten I recently took home. She must be growing quite impatient by now. I usually come home right after work and hurry to feed her, but today she'll remember what it is to be hungry."

"Oh. A kitten. How silly of me. Go, hurry to feed her." Bogdana felt a weight lifting from her shoulders. She realized she was attracted by Andrey and didn't want him to have a girlfriend. She was very pleased with the news about the kitten, and yet again saw Andrey in a different light. She had obviously been quite mistaken in her initial evaluation of him.

The young man's strategy was working like a charm.

Andrey excused himself once more and hurried home, and Bogdana was left alone. She stared in space and smiled, quite smitten; for a second, she had forgotten her fears and prejudice. But only a minute later, she stood up and left, as if someone had pinched her and brought her back to reality.

The next day, Andrey thanked her again and apologized for his sudden departure. But Bogdana acted aloof and cautious, just like she used to. For a while, Andrey lost faith in himself and his strategy, and called Gavril to share his worries. Gavril was truly amused by Andrey's distress, and told him to go on, always follow the plan closely, and be patient. Patience wasn't among Andrey's virtues, but his determination to win over Bogdana motivated him and gave him strength.

In the following week, Andrey passed his accounting exam successfully, and received a certificate attesting to his expertise in the area. His tutor even offered him a place in his accounting agency. He had no way of knowing that Andrey held a much more profitable position, and the course was just a part of his strategy.

Andrey used the opportunity to brag to Bogdana and thank her again for all her help, insisting, of course, that he couldn't have handled the exam without her. He asked her out to dinner, and to his great surprise, she accepted. The truth was, she missed him. They hadn't seen each other for a few days, and she feared she had driven him away with her stony behavior. She had started fantasizing about a dinner invitation, and there was no way she could refuse. She even said yes right away, without her usual quibbles and reservations, too afraid that Andrey may feel awkward and withdraw his invitation. Still, she didn't want him to drive her to the restaurant, so they agreed to meet there. He had the task of booking them a table.

That night, Andrey talked a lot, and Bogdana just listened and laughed at the funny fictional stories he entertained her with. A few times, he included references to some of Bogdana's favorite movies, which, of course, she recognized right away. The dinner went on smoothly;

Bogdana felt she was growing ever closer to Andrey, and thought perhaps she had found the right guy. She realized he had been hiding behind a mask until now, but in reality, he was a wonderful, slightly shy and very promising young man. And they had so much in common: they both loved cats, enjoyed the same movies and books. How were all these coincidences possible? *It's destiny*, she thought. While in fact, it was a cat-and-mouse game.

The night wore on, and they still had so much to say to each other. They laughed, looking deliriously happy.

At one point, Andrey sobered up and admitted, "You know, Bogdana, the more I get to know you, the more I like you. But my darling is pretty jealous, and I'm not sure she'll let you come close to me."

These words made Bogdana's smile dissolve like ice over a hot fire. She rose to Andrey's bait, reacting rashly and impulsively. "Your darling? And why do you even think I'd like to be in your life? I want to go home. You are just like all the others." Bogdana grabbed her coat and rushed to the exit.

Andrey followed her, and once out of the restaurant, he called, "What's gotten into you? Are you always so angry and aggressive?"

"Go away! Don't ever talk to me again!"

"I was just kidding. I wanted to make you laugh. I recently told you that my darling was a kitten, remember? I thought you'd find it funny if I mentioned that again."

Bogdana halted in her rush to get away. She felt awfully foolish. Yet again, she realized what a good person Andrey was, and how wrong she'd been. He reached her and took her in his arms, and the intense emotions brought tears to her eyes.

"Bogdana, if I had the chance to be with you, I'd never betray you, ever. I don't want you to be afraid of me. I'm no beast, I'm your friend. I suggest we went for a little walk, but would you wait for me to go back and pay the bill? I wouldn't want to be hunted by the police."

This time, Bogdana laughed at his joke. Of course, after ruining their perfect date with her ludicrous behavior, she was now ready to agree with anything Andrey suggested. She wouldn't want to embarrass herself any more, or test his willingness to be with her.

When Andrey returned from the restaurant, they walked arm in arm. The night grew even more romantic and beautiful. Out of Andrey's deception, a great love was born, and a real friendship. At the agency, people could hardly believe what was happening; even more so, when they were all invited to Bogdana and Andrey's wedding.

Andrey repeatedly met with Gavril to thank him for his invaluable advice. He asked his opinion on whether he should be honest with Bogdana and reveal how he managed to steal her heart. But the answer was no. Gavril told him to enjoy their wonderful moments together, and forget about the differences in their preferences and about the strategy. Gavril felt paternal towards this relationship, and not long after, he was invited to be the godfather of their first son, named after his mother – Bogdan.

Over time, Andrey grew more capable of identifying different personality types, which helped him a lot in his communication and in attracting new clients. Gradually, he became a chameleon like his mentor.

Now you've become experts in identifying personality types, let's go back to effective strategic sales and persuasive communication. I promised to tell you more about cross-selling, and now's the time to do so.

CROSS-SELLING

Cross-selling is an integral part of effective sales in the retail sector, without being limited to it. But these sales are often underrated, and companies don't pay them the attention they deserve.

Cross-selling involves the selling of products that are related to, but much less costly than the one being purchased, and sell at greater profit margins.

Such sales are often discussed, but not calculated in the bonus schemes of the sales reps; it's also very rare for them to be included in the monthly targets.

The truth is, cross-selling is invaluable because this type of expanding on the sale uses products with huge profit margins, worth no more than 10% of the value of the core product. Or, if we go back to the shoe store, when selling shoes for 150 leva, it's normal to cross-sell a product worth 5 to 15 leva – of course one with a great profit margin. In this particular case, such a product could be shoe shine, special soles, stockings, spare shoelaces, a polishing kit, etc.

However, if cross-selling sounds like a piece of cake to you, it hardly is so in real life. Sellers usually don't know how to properly offer a related product, and in 70% of the cases, their offer gets refused. For this technique to work, it needs excellent persuasive communication in place, motivated staff, and the element of bait, something to lure the client with.

Cross-selling is most effective when it's included in the main bonus scheme or has one of its own.

In general, offering a related product has no benefits. It can be purchased at any other time and from anywhere. There's nothing unique in such an offer, which makes it less alluring, which in turn does not bode well for the results. That's why sales assistants lose motivation and don't bother offering related products.

Store owners don't insist on it, because after all, these products only supplement their main business, and so the lack of an effective model leads to missed opportunities.

Perhaps you are wondering what there is to miss, so I'll give you an example.

For a client of mine, who owned a chain of retail stores, I developed a cross-selling system. It was included in the staff's bonus scheme, and added a significant amount. People were motivated to do things the way they were instructed to. The owner was worried that cross-selling could shift his employees' focus and make them more aggressive towards the customers, thus having a negative effect on his business. But he decided to trust me, and the system was implemented.

After all, we are speaking about a business model which is applied successfully all around the world, and everyone doing it right profits from it – or they wouldn't use it at all.

Over the year, the company made a little over 120,000 leva from cross-selling, for all 18 stores altogether. At first glance, that's not much, because that is about 10,000 a month for all stores, or 550 for a single store. But still, the profit from these 120,000 leva was over 85,000, because we are talking about products that sell at 300% or more above their original value. Half of this amount was given to the employees, who received an additional 40,000 to their remuneration.

The rest was money which the business had not made use of up to that point, and now it had 40,000 to 50,000 a year left for marketing.

But let's get back to the way you approach cross-selling so that it's effective.

Let's say there is a client at the cash desk, paying 120 leva for a pair of shoes. The shoes may be for the buyer or intended for another – this is an important information to have before attempting cross-selling.

Let's say you've been told the pair will be a gift.

"Would you like to add a shoehorn to your gift? We know from experience that people getting shoes cannot wait to try them on. They most likely won't have a shoehorn handy, and putting the shoes on may be difficult. To avoid an awkward situation, you'd better put this nice shoehorn in the box."

Possible answers: yes/no.

If the answer is yes:

"Wonderful, I'll add one the color of the shoes. That's great. But I forgot to tell you, if you also buy stockings from our new collection, you get the shoehorn for free. Would you like to take a look at them?"

If the answer is yes, we are now selling a more expensive product, and the cheaper one is given away for free.

The cheaper the products, the larger their profit margins. Let's say a shoehorn costs 0.40 leva and sells for

4 leva. It's sold for 1000% more than it's worth, but still, the profit amounts to only 3.60 lv.

The stockings from the collection mentioned cost 12 leva, only 300% more than they are worth, but we still have a profit margin of 8 leva, and even after subtracting the value of the shoehorn, we are left with 7.60, twice more than the profit form the shoehorn itself.

If the answer is no, we just close the deal after successfully cross-selling the shoehorn.

If the shoehorn was originally refused, it should be followed by another offer depending on the situation.

Usually, there's a script prepared, listing different cross-selling scenarios and covering most situations and possible answers.

When the client is purchasing something for personal use, it's even easier, because people see the world to their advantage – something we must always keep in mind.

You're probably getting bored with all these repetitions, but this fact is of utmost importance for creating effective advertising campaigns, below-the-line advertising, and whatever else you can come up within this sphere.

Each sale is a value exchange, and I already gave you several examples of a thing having positive value for one and negative for another. A deal must hold value for both consumer and company. Now I'll examine that complex exchange we call a sale a little closer.

THE SALE AS A
VALUE EXCHANGE

Let's say you'd like to lease your apartment. You've checked and you know that for such a high-end place, you could easily ask 1,000 leva a month. You find a person ready to pay such a rent, but they will be living with four dogs or four cats, doesn't matter which. Does this client's value change the moment you learn about their pets? It does. Even if they offered more, it's possible that you would refuse, because you wouldn't risk the animals ruining the furniture and fixtures, bothering the neighbors and so on.

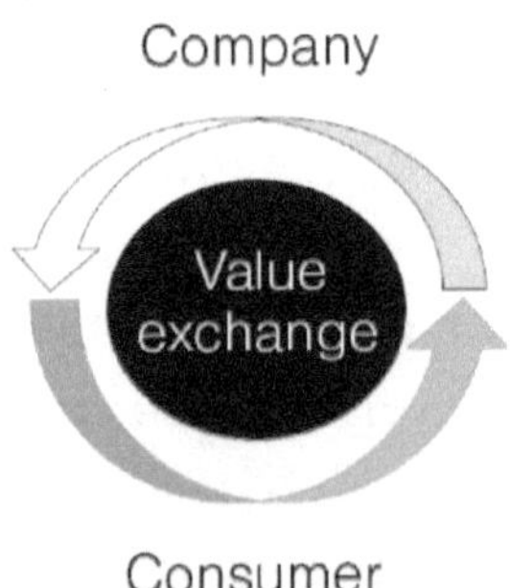

In short, value is relative, especially when it comes to offering services.

Imagine a high-end car being bought by a person not wealthy enough to afford it; they purchase it to gain prestige and self-confidence, although it's out of their league.

If the car breaks down in the first two or three years or needs some repairs, the client would be greatly annoyed. The yearly maintenance costs and insurance are already a serious burden to their limited budget, and small incidental expenses can cause them to shower the brand with abuse. It's highly likely that this person starts making his disappointment loud and clear over social media, ruining the brand's good name.

For wealthy customers, this same model is just another high-end car. They find it perfectly natural for it to break down and require repairs, to need upkeep and servicing. Some of them are not even aware how much these repairs or the regularly replaced consumables cost, because they have others to take care of it. That's why I say different clients hold different value for your business, and they should be carefully assessed before persuading them to buy.

The time invested in strategic sales could be too great if we cannot accurately assess the value of our potential client. And although I referred to a client, singular, what I said certainly applies to advertisement and sales strategies targeted at particular consumer groups.

If you plan on advertising a product, and you potential customer is one out of a thousand people, you cannot use the same method as when the potential customer is one out of ten. You need an entirely different communication and marketing strategy.

Good communication cannot be achieved by following a ready-made script; it's a frame of mind, and the result of long experience.

Take the following example. We have a client intending to by an exercise bike: a middle-aged woman, examining the sports equipment. Let's see what a mere consultant would say to her, compared to an experienced dealer, and you'll realize the huge difference in their approach.

Option #1: The client will be attended by a consultant. This consultant is a highly qualified woman who knows the technical features of all the equipment in great detail.

"Hello, madam. Are you looking for a bike for your personal use?"

"Hello. Yes, I'm going to be using it myself."

"Come with me, I'll show you the bikes with heavier flywheels, these weigh 13 pounds and are made for people up to 180 pounds." At that point, despite her best intentions, the consultant in fact tells the customer that she's too fat for the first bikes, and they'll break if she tries to mount them.

"Okay, where do you keep those for whales like me?"

"Oh, that's not what I meant. Here, these are the right ones for you. You can also monitor your blood pressure, calories burnt, distance covered, average speed, and pulse. You know, watching your pulse is every important; after 35, it's recommended that your pulse does not go over 160 beats a minute, or you run a health risk."

"Sure, I'll keep that in mind when I turn 35. I'm still 28."

So this is yet another unintentional offence despite the consultant's best intentions and desire to help the client. That's why it's necessary to ask questions and provide solutions and answers to the client's needs, not just talk, regardless of how much you know about the product in question.

Option #2: The client will be attended by an experienced salesperson.

"Hello, if you're going to use the bike yourself, you'd better get on and try it."

"Yes, it's for me."

"Then come with me, I'll show you the adult models. These are for children."

"Oh, really? I didn't know."

"No problem, it's my job to know and help you make the best choice. Tell me what you need. Why do you require an exercise bike?"

"Isn't it obvious? I must lose some weight."

"Okay, let me help you. Can you ride it every day for about an hour?"

"An hour a day, no. I planned on riding it from time to time. I have much work to do, and kids to take care of. I won't have time every day."

"It's great to exercise, but you know, some people ride such bikes every day with minimal improvement, while others achieve much more with less training. I've come to like you, so I'll tell you how, if you'd like to know?"

"Sure, please do."

"You should take these L-Carnitine tablets, they quicken the fat-burning process and will help you get great results even if you ride every other day. And because you're just starting, take these special vitamins, too. They'll raise your energy levels and boost your immune system. Do you think you can manage riding every other day?"

"I don't know. Knowing me, I'll probably be riding less frequently."

"Still, appetite comes with eating."

"Tell me about it, ha-ha."

"You have a great sense of humor, good for you."

"Thank you."

"I'm sure you'll notice results very soon, and it'll stimulate you. The envy of those around you will stimulate you even better. I know you women grow envious when a friend starts looking gorgeous, and you'll soon be a magnet for male gazes."

"Come on, you make me blush."

"Once you start, you shouldn't miss sessions, so you'd better take a fitness belt, too. When you have no time, put the belt on your belly and hips. It's on batteries, discharges electrical impulses and makes your muscles contract. You can even use it lying down. But don't give up on the bike, the belt is only for days when you can't ride. There are also waistbands which induce sweating, but I don't recommend them because you can easily get dehydrated. This here is the best combination."

"It's a lot of stuff, how much does it all cost?"

"Don't think about money, focus on yourself. Don't you think you deserve a little exercise and getting into shape?"

"I never indulge myself."

"People pay 10 leva per gym session and 10 more for a fitness instructor several days a week. Now this here is an investment! And it can be used by others, too."

"You're right, but the cost skyrocketed. Perhaps I could give up the belt."

"You could, but I would pay double to see the looks of some people in a month or two."

"Darn it, I'm taking everything. Now tell me, do I need anything else? Better buy it all in one go. You're absolutely right."

That's the difference between consulting and selling. Selling involves motivating, creating a need, exploiting emotions. Salespeople possess strong emotional intelligence and know how to react. In the example above, the salesperson cross-sold several expensive items, and at the same time motivated the client.

Now I'll share with you another business model which is seldom applied, but can greatly boost your sales. It's a discount method called cashback.

CASHBACK

In my other book, *Business above the Red Line*, I discuss this model in detail; here, I'll only mention the information related to our topic, persuasive communication.

You can use cashback at the time of purchase. You may give the client loyalty points or virtual currency that they can use for later purchases in your business.

Let's say, you're selling expensive clothes. A shirt from your new collection costs 300 leva. So you announce that all shirts bought in June will get 70% cash back. Meaning, everyone buying a shirt will get 70% of its value back in their account, or in this case, 210 leva. Thus, the customer pays only 90 leva for the shirt… or do they?

No, this is subtle manipulation, because you may give 210 leva back in your client's account, but at the time of purchase, they make a complete payment and hand you the entire amount of 300 leva. They can use the virtual money you gave them back for another purchase, but they pay the current one in full.

You can announce that virtual currency can be used only to buy products that are not already discounted or on offer, which guarantees that it will be used for goods with huge profit margins. Also, when paying with virtual money, clients cannot take advantage of the cashback scheme.

Thus, if said customer decides to buy another 300-leva shirt, they can use their virtual currency (210 leva), and pay only 90 leva in cash, without receiving a new bonus.

If we analyze the two purchases, the customer has bought two shirts and paid 390 leva in total. But they are left with a different impression. They believe they have paid only 90 leva for the first shirt, because you gave them 210 back, and then, they again pay only 90 leva for the second shirt, which is true, because the rest is drawn from their account.

Cashback is a useful tool for sales and promotional campaigns, as long as you have an adequate system for managing it; it should give your customers the option of monitoring their payments, loyalty points and purchase history.

ADVERTISEMENT BLINDNESS AND MARKET SHORT-SIGHTEDNESS

Did you know that, on average, we see about 20,000 advertisements a year? Ads are everywhere, it's all so colorful, and we are constantly showered by advertising slogans and invitations to make new and bargain purchases. Every day, companies offer us their unique and exceptional products and services, but we notice them less and less, because we suffer from the advertisement blindness syndrome. We don't see the ads, we don't remember them. We are so overwhelmed we can hardly remember even those we want to.

Sales assistants often have to try and find products that clients have seen on TV, but cannot remember how they are called.

This requires new approaches in both the advertising business and persuasive communication. It's more important than ever to work consistently with our current clients, because they are the best source of new ones. The lack of proper communication can lead not only to missed opportunities, but also to the potential loss of our loyal customers.

Unfortunately, the majority of companies are run by people who don't change a thing over the years of their "development". They don't introduce upgrades even when they see that business is getting slower. Instead of becoming more competitive, they lose their edge and advantage, which makes them ever more vulnerable. They believe the outflow of clients is caused by the economic crisis or by the emergence of malls, but truth is, their end is getting near due to their own market shortsightedness, which prevents them from employing creativity and thinking outside the box. They cut down on their marketing budgets – a thing that may increase their profits just as much as stopping their watches may save them time.

It's not natural to be outshined by a competitor who is only now establishing themselves in a sector you've been working in for more than twenty years, but it's in fact quite common.

When a new player enters the game, armed with creative thinking, a good team and a plan for their company's development for many years to come, they can easily outdo the ossified and shortsighted current players who do not intend to implement any changes, convinced in their long-standing expertise!

To be a successful seller, you must learn to look out the window, not only in the mirror.

The world is changing at lightning speed, and you must make use of all communication channels in the marketing mix. You must possess a wide range of knowledge and an excellent team in order to communicate successfully with the current and potential customers of your business.

You should avoid any advertising models based on pouring money in and waiting for deals to come automatically out. You should stop relying on your competitive advantage only, be it best price and/or location.

The way to go is to build networks of loyal customers and develop your brand, because it lends value to your products and services, and each sale is a value exchange. A powerful brand and good communication can give you unique competitive advantages.

But since views on loyal customers are pretty controversial, I'll spare a few paragraphs to explain. We must be aware of which client belongs to which group, in order to know how to communicate – if not with individual clients, then with their respective groups.

Since I took up marketing, I've been grouping clients into several categories:

» Potential customers
» Random customers
» Customers sent in by loyal customers
» Bargain hunters
» Loyal customers
» Brand advocates
» Former customers

Perhaps you're wondering, aren't there just customers? For me, there aren't; and there shouldn't be for any business that realizes the importance of continuing communication to help you strengthen the relationships with your clients, and turn them into loyal customers or brand advocates.

Bargain hunters are often considered as important as loyal customers, because they shop at a given store or chain of stores several times a year.

But if you use software that monitors not only the frequency, but also the type of purchases, you can easily identify bargain hunters. They are not loyal customers of yours. They like your products just as well as those of many other brands, and are likely to buy them only at a discount. They are on the lookout for clearance sales, and they only shop when the prices are low or there is a sample sale.

Once you isolate these customers, you can communicate with them in a different way. You can have special marketing and communications policies tailored to them. As you must have such policies towards your loyal customers and brand advocates.

Remember, brand advocates are a powerful marketing tool. They constantly introduce new customers to your business and do not allow criticism towards the brand. So be very attentive to them and keep the fire going. When you see someone defending your brand on social media or elsewhere, do something special for them. Express your gratitude in a way they would remember, and which will make them like you even more.

One loyal customer, on average, can bring up to seven new customers to your business in a year. A brand advocate can bring up to fifteen.

Regardless of the scope of your business, you should find a way to classify your customers not only by type and color, but also according to how active they are, and how many others they refer to you.

LOYALTY AND REFERRAL
PROGRAM

Now is the time to discuss referrals, which are extremely important for the development of your network of loyal customers, and for persuasive communication.

There's nothing better than a friend of yours convincing you about the advantages and uniqueness of a given product or service. They have no reason to lie and nothing to gain, and are themselves customers of the brand in question. Almost all of my clients in the last seven or eight years have come to me after a recommendation from a satisfied client of mine.

When it comes to persuasive communication, it may include anything leading to good brand reputation and an increase in sales. That's why, if your business allows for it, don't hesitate to create a referral and reward program for those recommending you.

Let's say you own a restaurant. You could issue customer loyalty cards, making clients part of your loyalty program. Every time they visit your restaurant, they'll check in their card, and when you collect enough data and make sure they visit regularly and spend a decent amount, you can make them an offer. You may give them coupons for a one-time 30% discount, to offer their friends and colleagues, as long as those people have never been to your restaurant before – in other words, the coupons will target only new customers.

Thus, when they offer a coupon to a friend, they are doing that friend a favor, giving them a serious discount. And as you can already guess, when a loyal customer offers this coupon to a friend, it will be accompanied by persuasive communication. Your customer will share with their mate what a nice restaurant yours is, how tasty the food is, how often they themselves visit, and what a good idea it would be for that person to go as well.

Few people would believe such claims in an ad, but said by a friend, they acquire much more value.

You can proceed in this way, or motivate your loyal customer even more, offering them a reward for a job well done. You can offer them an additional 3% off for the entire year if at least five of the coupons you handed them get used by new customers. Which means that these coupons must have a unique serial number, associated with their file in your loyalty program, and once a new customer pays their bill using the coupon, the system should automatically record it in your loyal customer's file.

When I presented such referral systems at my trainings, many attendees posed questions along the lines of, "I don't understand. Why shouldn't I give such coupons to everybody with a loyalty card? Why do I need to wait and collect data, and only make the offer after being sure they are regular customers?"

You shouldn't give away coupons to all your customers. You have to be sure that the ones you approach really like you and come repeatedly. It's important that these people know how to promote you, that they can recommend specific dishes, desserts or drinks. It will make them more convincing and demonstrate to their friends that they really are regulars, and know the menu, atmosphere and service well. For this to work, the loyal customers must have come to the restaurant at least seven times before you approach them with your offer. Such an approach guarantees that at least four out of every ten people you present with the offer will agree, and at least one out of those four will give out between five and seven coupons to their friends and acquaintances.

If you start offering coupons to everyone on their first or second visit, you risk being on the losing side. It's like planting corn and harvesting it green. It won't do even for fodder.

Some may say, "What's the big deal, I'll hand coupons to everyone, they may pass them on or not, it's all the same to me." But such careless thinking won't result in an increase in sales.

Imagine having a hundred customers coming to the restaurant for the second time, and making them this offer. They don't know the menu yet, they may not have even tried the specialties, and you haven't given them the free bottle of wine you give away at the fifth visit. You haven't celebrated any special occasion with them; your relationship is still in the bud. So you shouldn't do any business with them. They are not regulars yet, and you need more time to "woo" them before they are ready for such an offer. You share no emotional connection yet.

Still, you rush into this step, and fifty of them agree. Out of these fifty, forty give coupons to family and friends. And if that sounds good, you must know it's not, because they are not good promoters yet. They don't know your restaurant, your menu, and haven't come to love you. So their persuasive communication won't be effective enough, they won't be able to answer any questions arising, and in the end, they won't bring in many new customers. And if you are still thinking "It's no big deal", I'll tell you that this means great losses from missed opportunities. You've shot all your bullets too early, and to no avail.

If you let the relationship develop and make the offer at a later stage, you'll witness much better results. Then your clients will be able to promote you very convincingly to their friends and coworkers, and many of them will also become customers of yours.

Selling requires lots of patience, effort, analysis, psychology, and consumer knowledge.

ADDED **VALUE**

Each one of these can meet your need for a new T-shirt in exactly the same way. They all may be made of the same fabric and have the same quality of manufacture, but their prices are totally different.

Let's say a plain white T-shirt costs 5 leva. A printed image can increase its price by 200% or even 300%, because it adds emotion, but it couldn't make its worth equal to that of a branded T-shirt.

People who buy branded goods in fact buy social status, self-respect, power, emotions, etc. This is all value added by the brand, for which you have to work constantly and spare no investment. The brand is the face of the company's entire mission and principles; it's much more than just an image that have to be advertised often enough for it to stick in consumers' minds.

Of course, a brand needs firm support from the entire team responsible for the workings of a company, in order to retain its top market position and win over even more consumers.

Those employees in direct contact with the end consumer can either lend or strip value off the brand. Here, persuasive and adequate communication matters more than ever.

But most of what I've shared so far relates to cases when the customers are there, they've already noticed us, and we just need to sell them something. The problem of attracting new customers remains, so in the following chapter I'll talk about ways to focus consumers' attention on our products and services, to strike a deal and make them part of our network of loyal customers.

BUILDING A NETWORK OF
LOYAL CUSTOMERS

If you'd like for your efforts to grow the business, as well as for your advertisement campaigns, to bear most fruit, you must read the following passages very carefully. They will disclose the secret of building a network of loyal customers.

Regardless of the nature of your business, it would be extremely difficult and highly ineffective to always keep trying to attract new clients.

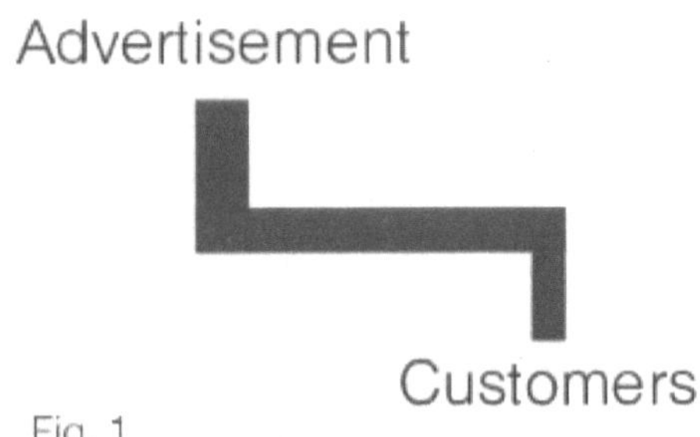

The illustration above shows a lowly effective advertising method. On one hand, we pour money into advertising and hope for it to bring in customers, and on the other, we count on our profit to cover the marketing costs. This model relies on constant proceeds from new clients, without even attempting to grow a network of loyal ones.

Business profits often come only after closing a second deal with the same client, because more often than not, the costs of "creating" a new client cannot be covered by the first deal. That's why you should avoid one-time deals if your business allows for repeated ones. You'd better build networks of loyal customers by working with your current clients – they are a constant source of new ones and will help you create a strong brand, which in turn will lend **more and more value to your products and services**.

You're going to be very disappointed if you expect clients to start buying as soon as they see your ad. Few consumers would ever do so, especially if they hear about you for the first time.

That's why, an effective strategy would be to implement a sales funnel through which the consumer passes until the time is right for a deal. It illustrates the different communication stages.

SALES FUNNEL

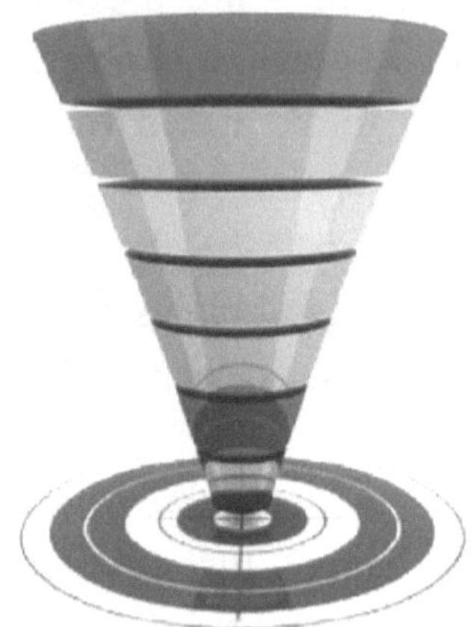

Fig. 2 Sales Funnel

Passing through the different levels of the funnel takes time and resources, and requires a lot of effort, knowledge and patience. On the other hand though, it achieves wonderful results. So what is that funnel each consumer must pass through?

Let's say, you'd like to advertise your beauty salon, and to do so, you make a series of instruction manuals available for free on your website. At the Hair Care page consumers can download the manual for achieving perfect hair. A similar manual for perfect skin can be downloaded from the Skin Care page. And finally, yet another manual for perfect manicure and pedicure can be found on the Nail Care page.

Once someone downloads one of these manuals, it means they are actively interested in caring for their hair, skin or nails, and you have to keep communicating with them on the subject. This communication shouldn't be limited to emails, but exploit all communication channels available. This customer should be an integral part of your Facebook, Instagram and Google AdWords audiences. All the information you've written and posted on the subject should reach them. Thus, in time, they'll come to regard you as a strong brand and trust you, which is vital for effective sales.

Of course, that means creating expectations that you must fulfil when said consumer decides to become a client of yours. Otherwise you'll cause disappointment, and the outcome won't be to your liking.

*Taking budget in consideration, every business should determine the appropriate **marketing mix** which will be the basis of your communication and advertisement strategy – a must-have. As "marketing mix" is often used to refer to various communication channels, I'd like to explain it in a few words.*

The marketing mix is related to the implementation of a marketing strategy, and it is not limited to the channels for communication and promotion of a product, but also includes the product/service itself, its price and packaging, and the distribution channels.

It's extremely important how your product looks, how it is perceived by consumers, how it is positioned – or how you wish for it to be positioned on the market. Also, what audience your marketing strategy is targeted at. Don't think that an ad on a popular media site like Facebook is enough for a successful marketing campaign. You must find a way to grab consumers' interest and make them come in contact with your business.

Once contact is established, you'd better find out their needs, the reasons why they'd come to you and how you can be of service to them. It's necessary to communicate with these consumers for a long enough period, and in an appealing enough way, to make them clients of yours.

If you have a funnel, you must plan how to take consumers through all of its levels so that they emerge as satisfied customers. Then you must work with them, making them visit you regularly, sympathize with you, trust you and recommend you to their acquaintances who may also become clients of yours.

Perhaps now you're thinking, "Easier said than done". It's what everybody wants for their business, and struggles to accomplish. But what's the best way to go about it?

Let's take a look at several different strategies for attracting and retaining customers, which I hope will make it easier to understand. I'm sure once you've read them, you would be able to easily apply what you've learned to your business. But first, I'll tell you how to subtly press the client through limitations, and how to shift focus.

PRESSING THE CLIENT
THROUGH LIMITATIONS

People don't dream of things they can afford, but they often buy exactly that after being consulted. Consultants usually follow an established scenario that never varies.

Staying firmly in the box can never lead to extraordinary and unexpected results, so you'd better think outside it and be creative.

Let me give you an example for pressing the customer in the retail sector: a clothing store. Consultants often use the classic approach towards hesitating customers, informing them that this is the last item left. "I just want you to know that there are no more dresses available from this model, so I can't guarantee you that it'll still be here tomorrow" or "I'd recommend thinking your purchase over carefully, but this is the last pair left." The second one is a bit more original, but we can also appeal to the customer's selfishness for additional motivation.

It's much better to take the focus away from the client's hesitation to buy, and act as if they'd already made the decision. "Would you mind taking the jacket from the window, because the last one of your size is reserved? We put that one on the dummy earlier today, it's not been there long."

Our question makes it clear that there are no more jackets available, and someone has even reserved the last one. The information is mentioned in passing, creating a slight sense of agitation, and at the same time, prickling one's selfishness. It's entirely possible that the client concedes to buy the jacket only if they're given the "reserved" one. Thus, they'll feel victorious. They'll be taking another person's jacket, and will be able to brag about it, which makes them feel triumphant. And we'll indulge them, giving them the "reserved" jacket, and taking the one from the window to keep for the other person who allegedly wanted it.

In such a scenario, everyone will be pleased – as long as our client is not Yellow. They'd never agree to take what belongs to another, but in the circumstances, they wouldn't mind buying the one from the window, especially when stimulated by a compliment.

AN EXAMPLE OF DEVELOPING A CLIENT NETWORK

BUILDING A CLIENT NETWORK FOR A NEWLY-LAUNCHED RESTAURANT

It's much easier to create a successful image when starting from scratch, than to improve the image of a business that already has a bad reputation. But of course, it's not impossible.

I rely on the same principle when training new salespeople. I believe it's easier to write on a blank sheet, so I prefer training people who still haven't acquired damaging habits or learned the trade from an aggressive dealer.

Imagine you are assigned the task to develop a restaurant with a hundred seats, which is about to open. You have to build a client network as soon as possible, because the restaurant has great fixed expenses.

In most cases, new restaurants are understaffed. The reason being, clients are scarce – and since clients are scarce, what's the point of keeping more than one cook and one waiter at a time? After all, as business grows, the number of staff can grow, too. It's a common mistake which automatically leads to a bitter ending.

And if you're wondering what this has to do with communication and marketing, the answer is, a lot. Marketing, advertising and communication are a family that affect the entire sales process. If there's something fishy in the way a business is structured that will affect its image or communication, it will affect sales, too.

I've also seen the opposite scenario, a restaurant launching with enough staff to keep visitors satisfied and not delay their orders, but it couldn't attract enough clients for a long time due to the lack of effective marketing strategy. It was overwhelmed by the monstrous expenses and went belly up. Truth is, things are complex and interrelated; all the elements must be there from the very beginning, and the management and communication systems must be built even before opening. You must have enough staff to serve your clients at decent speed, but at the same time, you cannot afford to slowly grow your customer base.

If you offer top quality and believe you've made something intriguing, you must be quick to make as many people aware of it as possible.

Obviously, every client who visits will tell a friend, and gradually, in the course of several years, the restaurant will fill up to capacity, but it would cost the owners too much. That's why it's imperative to create a marketing and communication strategy from the very beginning. Calculating it in the initial investment is much more cost-effective than waiting for clients to gradually notice you.

A SAMPLE STRATEGY
FOR DEVELOPING A NEWLY-LAUNCHED RESTAURANT

Before going into detail about this strategy, I'd like to point out that this is only one of several possible approaches. And since my previous example about the loyalty and referral program involved a restaurant, I'll use one again; I believe you could easily apply everything I mention to your own business and marketing strategy.

» Restaurant launch

We have to inform as many people as possible about the event. It will include numerous surprises and free tokens for all visitors, and they will be asked to make a reservation in advance. In this way, we can guarantee that there will be no empty tables, and at the same time, no guests will find themselves without one. Such an event is not intended to bring in profit, but to promote the restaurant. It must be visited by as many people as possible over the first month, so that it becomes known and is always fully booked in the future.

With a successful communication strategy, it's possible that the number of people willing to come is much higher than the hundred seats available. In such a situation, many managers will smile and apologize to those wanting to come, saying the restaurant is all booked. Perhaps they'll add "We'll be happy to have you another time", but that is quite insufficient and does not justify all the money invested in promoting the launch.

Once all tables are booked, we should apologize to anyone new wishing to attend the event, and extend an invitation. We should suggest that they book a table for another day right away, adding that it comes with a bottle of excellent white or red wine, courtesy of the restaurant. Without waiting for an answer, we should mention that all tables are already booked for the coming Friday and Saturday after 6 p.m.

In this way, we shift the focus from "would they like to come again" to "when will it be possible to", because our restaurant fills in very fast. And don't forget about the thoughtful gift, which is in no way tied to any amount spent, because that would be rather tactless.

In these circumstances, the potential customer may be unwilling to book for various reasons. Perhaps they would like to visit exactly on the dates we mentioned as fully booked – and here we should be wary of making another mistake.

Many managers would demonstrate making an effort to find seats in the allegedly full restaurant, and it could come back to bite them later. Imagine pretending to have miraculously dug up seats in a fully booked restaurant, but when the visitors come, they find the place half-empty. What would they think? If you decide to play a role, pretend success to achieve success. You must be an excellent script writer and a master of persuasive communication.

No matter how the conversation ends, we've offered a courtesy and should make an effort to get the name and confirm the number of the customer even if they refuse to book. If they do, we'd have reason enough to ask for all the data we need.[3]

If the client is unwilling to book a table at a later date, we should ask why: because they would like to visit on the days when we are fully booked, because they are not sure when they'll be able to come, because they would like to consult with their partner, or...? This information must be put down and used strategically during follow-up conversations.

With the launch in motion and the restaurant full, our visitors are enjoying delicious food and excellent service. By default, each meal ends with a fine dessert, courtesy of the house, and a short survey. Very short indeed: a few closed questions, one open-ended one, and text fields to enter one's name, phone number and email. Filling in the survey entitles the client to a free bottle of wine, as long as their next reservation is made by the end of the month.

You may wonder why we bother collecting names, numbers and emails when these people have already booked a table, providing us with their names and numbers. It is to acquire their emails; and furthermore, the person booking usually does not come alone, but brings a number of acquaintances, friends and family, whose contact details may be of great use to us. By means of this short survey, we could determine whether we have met our customers'

---

[3] Avoid asking for email addresses on the phone because they can be easily misheard. You'd better leave the collection of emails for the visit itself, or for digital marketing where the client is asked to provide and confirm their data on their own.

expectations and what aspects we should consider improving.

When filling in a survey that is not anonymous, people are prone to overlook little deficiencies as long as they have had a good time. So it is important to encourage them with a phrase like, "Please be completely honest and do not spare us anything as it is vital for our future." Introduced in this manner, the survey is bound to collect more authentic answers and constructive criticism, if there is any.

Of course, the visitors of a launch are hardly enough to provide constant occupation of all the tables in a restaurant. That's why, in addition to the follow-up communication with all the evening's guests, we need to organize a series of events attracting more and more customers. When planning new self-funded events aimed at increasing foot traffic, it is not necessary to invite people who have already attended such events. They could be invited of course, but it is not mandatory.

As I already noted, the publicity costs of such events, coupled with the compliments' prices, would probably curtail profit, so it is preferable for these occasions to be frequented by as many new customers as possible, while those who have already visited and provided their contact details will receive other invitations and offers.

And presuming we have managed to organize four or five such events in the first month following our launch, thus attracting four to five hundred people, it is now time to reduce the number of events bringing new customers, and focus on working with our current ones, those who already know us. We must strike while the iron is hot, meaning they should not be allowed to forget us and the great time they had here.

By employing a little cunning, we could know much more about our customers than they would imagine. With the help of the waiting staff, based on food and drinks ordered, we could note in a customer's file what food they chose from the options provided, and whether they consumed alcohol and what kind. And if they did, we could note what quantity they drank; it may sound excessive, but it is important. It is also important to know what tip they gave. All that data accumulates in customer profiles, which help us create a network of loyal customers. It is worth mentioning here that my agency's slogan is exactly that – a formula for loyal customers.

To me, customers are the bosses of my business!

Carefully selected data will be of great use in our follow-up communication.

By virtue of possessing data about all customers, we have made use of the advantages of digital environment, which I will examine in more detail further on in the book. These people are now audiences we can target with our advertising and content marketing, and by other means aimed at developing emotional engagement to the brand.

And since emotional engagement requires effort, we have to start extending invitations to people who have visited us a few weeks ago and haven't come back since. Now it's a matter of creativity to come up with an unusual invitation. It may be extended via phone, email or social networks, or even using all of these channels. It all depends on the proposal itself.

Let's say, we've planned an evening with a famous patisserie chef who is going to prepare a special selection of his best desserts for our patrons to sample for free. Or we could offer a special wine selection for every table of four or more.

It's all a matter of strategy. The important thing is for customers to come and feel satisfied, so that they get into the habit of visiting our restaurant, and bringing in new customers.

» Creating a loyalty program

In one of the previous chapters, I already discussed how you can apply a loyalty and referral program to a restaurant, so you now know the advantages of such a program.

» Drawing up a lunch menu

» Drawing up a dinner menu

» Offering bonuses, e.g.: for every check over 200 leva – free taxi

» Special offers on holidays: valid not only for national holidays, but also for name days

» Special offers for birthday celebrations

» Special family deal

» Special corporate deal

» Special offers for "dead" time periods when the place is usually deserted

» Building partnerships for customer exchange, etc.

» Symbiotic positioning

» Referral system, etc.

An excellent cuisine and service, combined with all the ideas above and padded by a successful communication and marketing strategy, will manage to fill up the restaurant in no time.

I know you may feel slightly disappointed that not all elements of this strategy are described in detail, but business growth is not the focus of this book. My aim here is to talk more about the power of communication, and about direct sales. My other book, *Business above the Red Line,* is focused on business growth; it contains lots of detailed examples, and there you can follow the process of successful business development step by step.

And since I mentioned surveys in the example above, which seem quite easy to do at a glance, I'd like to talk a bit more about this delicate form of communication. You must take into account that more often than not, the person drawing up the survey designs not only the questions, but their answers as well.

Let me give you an example.

Four different countries did a survey to establish how many people were willing to donate their organs if they died in a crash or similar circumstances. The question was phrased in two possible ways. One of the variants received 90% negative responses, while the other got over 80% positive ones.

If you are already wondering how that is possible, and why such a great difference, it's all due to the different phrasing.

In the first case, people were asked **if they were willing to donate their organs**, and in the second, **if they minded donating their organs**. This seemingly minor difference turned out to be extremely important.

That's why, before designing surveys, you must have a clear aim. You have to know what information you want out of the consumer, and phrase the questions in such a way that they'll elicit the answers you need in order to communicate further with this person and turn them into a loyal customer.

But let's set surveys aside and concentrate on the possibilities of the marketing mix, and how to make most use of it for the purposes of our business.

As I already mentioned, we're living in a time of advertisement blindness, and it's crucial to create a strategy for constant contact with our customers that will keep them interested and win over their loyalty.

Marketing and communication are often underestimated, and managed by people without enough experience and expertise in the field. This science is considered easy as pie, and almost every manager, not to say every employee, believes themselves a marketing expert, which doesn't bode at all well for their business and its growth. Even writing a single article is not an easy task, let alone creating and managing an entire marketing strategy.

But of course, you are not one of those people; if you're reading this book, you must be aware of the power of good communication and the need for expertise and professionalism.

To achieve results, every detail of your advertisement and communication strategy has to be well thought-out and evaluated by experts. Only then would marketing expenses be justified and achieve good business results. Only then would your brand lend an added value to the products and services you offer.

MARKETING AND PERSUASIVE COMMUNICATION IN THE 21ST CENTURY

Busy lifestyle, over-saturated markets and the abundance of advertisements robbed businesses of the possibility to advertise and organize marketing and communication campaigns without serious expertise.

We have quick and easy access to information, so we can look up any price or other details we are uncertain about. In mere minutes, we can verify the reputation of a given person or business.

We are flooded by articles, so we read the headlines only and scan the text; if the headline works, we check out the rest, and if it is written well, by a professional copywriter, we read it through. If it ends with a call for action, it gets shared on social media, gaining even more popularity thanks to viral marketing.

It turns out that even the writing of a single article, part of your content marketing, is governed by numerous rules.

In the following paragraphs, I'll take a look at most communication channels that you may use. I'll explain how to be convincing and effective in the way you present yourself to consumers. There's also a special chapter called

"Reading the signs", which contains lots of examples to help you hone this skill.

WRITING ARTICLES, PR TEXTS AND USEFUL PIECES FOR ATTRACTING AUDIENCES

Before showing you how to win over customers through the parallel use of several tools from the marketing mix, I'll tell you more about each of them separately, and then we'll combine them in a well-planned marketing and communication strategy. The way I'll introduce it, permission marketing is definitely a mixture between marketing and PR.

Less than 10% of the information that reaches us on a daily basis is unique – everything else we see all over the media, is a slightly altered copy or a translation from another language.

Few people realize how powerful a publication can be, and what advantages unique and intriguing content can have as long as it is valuable to the reader.

I often come across companies who publish PR texts in powerful media, but achieve only a fraction of the results such publications can bring about.

To be effective and not mere padding, every publication should be part of an entire marketing and/or communication strategy, as well as be strategically composed itself. It should keep the reader invested all the time, not letting them scan the subheadings and bolded lines alone.

Statistically speaking, a reader spends less than 60 seconds on an average publication. If the average time spent reading your text is 90 seconds or more, this is a good result. A period of two minutes would be very good, and a period of three or more – excellent. And if with printed media it's impossible to measure those times, with digital ones it's easy, and in my opinion, mandatory. Use the power of digital media to analyze your texts.

Start with the headline: the head of your publication is what matters most. The headline determines how many times the article will be read, or at least how many times it will be opened; whether it will be read through depends on its content, i.e. the body of the article.

To ascertain the power of your headline and learn to write loud and catchy ones, you can use a headline analyzing tool.

Certain tools allow you to test several headlines before letting your article roam the web. The differently titled versions will be shown to different readers, and you'd get feedback about which headline works best.

Imagine you are planning a text which will cost a certain amount to be written, then more to be published on a leading media site, and even more to help it reach a wider audience. It should matter to you how many people will read it; you'd want to reach as many people from your target audience as possible. That's why you should test your headlines to see which get more hits and which are less attractive.

You will get feedback showing what percentage of those seeing your headline have clicked on it and visited your page with the article. In this way, you'll know which headline is most catchy, and in time learn to write better ones.

Let me give you an example.

"New technology for safe teeth whitening"

"Revolutionary discovery: new technology for safe teeth whitening"

"Get your teeth four shades whiter in a month with new safe technology"

In your opinion, which of these three headlines works best? Which one would you choose?

The third headline is the most powerful.

Imagine the following figures: out of a thousand people reached, your first headline gets ten hits, the second one – fifteen hits, and the third one – thirty-five hits. If you don't bother checking how strong your headline is, you risk missing serious traffic towards your publication. And if its content is top quality and it's more than a catchy headline, viral marketing can increase its popularity several times over.

The content, the body, determines the benefits. If you present an attractive body, you'd be read and shared. That's easy to achieve if your article, despite containing valuable information, is written well. At strategic points where the reader may abandon it or skip content, **you should put hooks**. This means occasionally inserting phrases that keep the reader's attention and interest. *E.g. Keep reading, and you'll find out how to spend three times less money on internet advertising than your competitors!* That's what we call a hook sentence. Even if the reader has decided to skip the rest, who wouldn't like to pay less? We always think to our advantage, we'd like to be stronger and better, so we'd never wish to pay more than our competitors.

Depending on the topic and nature of your content, you should apply everything that you learned so far to craft appropriate hooks which will keep your reader awake until the end of the article, and won't let them skip content you consider important. If your topic allows it, you should end the piece with a call for action that will help it reach a wider audience: *If you find this article useful, please share it with your friends.*

Keep in mind that even an unconvincing call for action works better than none at all.

BUILDING AUDIENCES

The power of digital marketing, its strategic use for constantly staying in touch, and permission marketing

Digital marketing really offers endless possibilities, and you'd better know them well and use them when communicating with current and potential customers. Hardly any strategy does not involve digital activities, and more often than not, they are predominantly digital.

Knowing the technical side is not enough. You must learn to apply all functionalities strategically, and use them for effective communication.

Clients must be constantly contacted, be they actual or potential. But your current and potential customers require different strategies for communication and constant contact.

And since many people associate regular contact with aggressive SPAM messages, I'd like to point out that's not what I mean; I refer to professional communication and marketing.

Let's get back to our restaurant. Here's what we have at our disposal:

» webpage

» Facebook business page

» Instagram profile

» Pinterest profile

» Foursquare profile

» Tweeter profile

» LinkedIn profile

» Google + profile

» our customers' emails and phone numbers

» ad account in Google AdWords

» excellent skills in organizing webinars

Of course, you may have many other profiles, but in this case I'll stick to these. What matters is not to have dozens of profiles and use all communication channels, but to make good use of those you consider the most effective. I won't elaborate on all of the channels above, as the topic is huge enough for an entire book. Still, I'd like to focus on how to build audiences, how to design your webpage, and how to communicate with consumers via email.

What we need for our marketing strategy:

» to have the emails of potential customers

» to know what audiences have visited our website, and their behavior

» to know what people engage with our publications

» to have referrals from current customers

» and above all: we need lots of customers to fill up the restaurant at all times

WEBPAGE AND COMMUNICATION

Quite often, business owners draw up the project for their webpage, and it is then implemented by web designers. This may seem perfectly okay to you, but it is not. You shouldn't design a website without consulting a marketing expert. If designed well, this site may be a constant source of new emails of people interested in your business, and thus potential customers.

The site may strategically "walk" visitors around your well-organized content, collecting valuable information about their behavior. It's important to know what message you'd like to share with your customers, and to do so in the best possible way.

Think about consumer experience and psychology. What would you like to achieve? What would you like consumers to do?

Let's say your strategy for attracting potential customers involves downloading a free manual or book from your site, as long as they leave their names and email addresses.

A tiny difference in the way this information is presented can lead to radically different results.

Your book has a catchy title. Let's say your website audience consists of people who take interest in business, marketing and sales. You title is *13 Strategies for Attracting and Retaining Customers*. Many people would like to learn those strategies and will download the book, but will it live up to their expectations?

At that point, people are usually disillusioned and greatly disappointed. That's why you have to know what you want and what you're going for, and that' can't be simply collecting emails via offering a book with an appealing title and substandard content.

To lend value to yourself and/or your brand, you have to match consumer expectations or even exceed them. And if your title is so bombastic, what's inside the book must also be first-rate and useful; only then would follow-up marketing achieve good results.

After you've done your best and really have something to offer consumers, you must present the information in the most captivating way:

Read it for free!
Name:
Email:

Is that enough? For the information to be adequate and effective, always take care to include the following:
» an irresistible offer
» added urgency
» relevance
» clarity
» anxiety, concern – the sense that the client will miss out if they don't act now
» eliminating distractions
» action

In the example here, you have an irresistible offer in the form of a book with 13 strategies to attract and retain customers, but you lack other elements which, if present, would improve your results.

Let's add some anxiety, a sense of urgency, by telling clients they may miss out if they don't hurry.

First 100 downloads are free!
Name:
Email:

It looks good, but it may get even better. We can add a price and then explain that the first 100 downloads are free, then add a call-to-action button: Download here!

We can test which variant works best, seeing how consumers react if presented with the various scenarios. There are tools that record consumer behavior, so that you can see which content attracts their attention and which – not so much. Then you'll know not only how to structure your irresistible offer, but also where best to put your CTA button.

First 100 downloads are free!
Name:
Email:
Download here!

First 100 downloads are free!
Name:
Email:
Click here! 87/100

Thus it's even easier to see that there are only 13 free downloads left before the offer expires. Everything is a matter of strategy and analysis.

Some people may not approve of the last trick, claiming consumers shouldn't be misled; someone may visit the page again later and see it still says 87/100. This is entirely possible, but I don't believe anyone will be mad with you for misleading them to download a wonderful book with 13 strategies for attracting customers. After all, you've employed such a strategy yourself, much cleverer than sending unsolicited messages (SPAM).

In fact, to avoid any disappointment, you yourself may urge the consumer to return to the page and see the numbers 87/100 have not changed. That may be the first of your promised 13 strategies. Remind the consumer that this very strategy helped you convince them to download your free book.

But let's get back to our webpage's audience.

What's an audience, how do we build it and what's its role in marketing and follow-up communication?

When you have a Facebook and a Google AdWords profile, you can generate codes and put them on your site, just like the code of Google Analytics, and through the so-called cookies, register people who visited the site or specific pages on it, and did specific actions.

Let's say you have a beauty salon with a very successful online presence thanks to your site. On your webpage, you've listed what services you offer, you've given customers to download a free manual with hair care/skin care advice, and you've put those tracking codes.

You can build an audience of:

» people who have read a specific article

» people who have visited a specific section of your services

» people who have visited the contacts page with the salon's address

» all visitors of the site

Moreover, the emails you collected from those who downloaded your manual, can be turned into another audience to target with your services.

By building different audiences, you can tailor specific ads or information to them, approach them daily and have your brand leave a strong impression in their minds.

It's not necessary to shower them with ads and prompts to buy alone. You can also promote other publications, seminars or events of yours, present them with special offers or whatever you like. It's a low-budget opportunity to communicate with audiences who are already familiar with your brand; I'm not talking about cold calling here. Of course, you should use the collected emails for email marketing as well. But as I mentioned cold calling, let me explain the difference between "cold" and "warm" calling.

Cold calling involves approaching a consumer who has no knowledge of you and the products or services you offer. They have not heard much about your brand, or have heard nothing at all.

However, when you communicate with consumers and keep constantly in touch with them, you warm up your relationship and gradually build up trust. Thus, you won't be cold calling them any longer, which guarantees more effective sales.

EMAIL MARKETING

Many people confuse this with the sending of unsolicited messages known as SPAM. This type of communication has a negative effect on your image, and respectively, on your brand.

Each action that can harm the brand had better be avoided, since, as I already mentioned, your brand lends value, and your actions shouldn't reduce its effectiveness, nor should you annoy your potential customers with unprofessional behavior.

True email marketing is based on communicating with people who have agreed to receive email updates from us, and are always free to terminate their subscription.

Having specific lists, we can send them useful information in the form of training marketing, and from time to time, a deal or an invite for particular action.

When we send an email, we should always be aware how many people have taken the action we've hoped they would.

If I continue my beauty salon example, we may send an email with information about a new procedure, or explaining about our new nail printer machine. The email contains a catchy title, pictures and an invitation to click a button and learn more by watching the video on a specific page of our website.

It's very important to know which people visited the site by clicking the email link.

Most platforms for email marketing provide such statistics and you may monitor the effects of every email: which links have been clicked, how much time visitors have spent on a particular page, and what actions they have taken afterwards.

Let's say, out of the 500 people you approached during your campaign, 30 visited your website and watched the video. You can immediately compile a new list of those 30 emails and send them a new message with an attractive personalized offer. Thus, you'll make these people feel special.

*People nowadays have too varied a choice and too little time, which drives them towards decisions based primarily on **trust: the most powerful weapon of a brand.***

You are well aware that products are made in factories, while brands are made in people's heads, so you must invest more in people. You are in the business with people, whom you supply with goods and services, not in the business with goods which you offer to people. Nowadays, everybody wishes to be special and receive individual attention, as well as personalized products and services. Use the power of marketing to create this effect in the consumers' minds.

Email marketing provides you with another unique opportunity – an automatic answer that doesn't look at all automatic. You can program your platform in such a way that after every file download, or every message left through the contact form, the system sends an automatic, though personalized response.

Let's say Mrs. Ivanova downloads the free manual from your site. She is obliged to fill in her name and email address. Then you can have 10 emails scheduled to be sent every week, guiding Mrs. Ivanova through the sales funnel.

First email, two days later:

Hello, Mrs. Ivanova, we hope the manual you downloaded from our site was useful. We'd appreciate your feedback. We'd also like to give you some additional useful information. Please, follow the link below.

Second email, three more days or a week later:
Hello, Mrs. Ivanova ...

And so on, the emails continue arriving on schedule, following a prearranged script, until at one point there comes an invitation to buy or a call to another desirable action.

The automatic nature of this process guarantees that nobody will be skipped, and everybody will receive the necessary portion of individual care and attention.

Of course, it's your responsibility to monitor whether a person interacts with the email and the links in it every time, or has stopped reading what you send them. If that is the case, you must revert to plan B and capture the customer's interest by other means.

Now imagine a client has downloaded something from your site, so they're the target of email marketing, and at the same time you've added them to a particular audience and show them ads – for example, new Facebook posts or other advertisements in the Google AdWords partner network.

The effect will be spectacular. This person will see your presence everywhere; you'll be communicating with them differently through the different channels, but wherever they go, they'll be overwhelmed by interesting and useful information and tempting offers, all coming from you. There's no way that they don't come to love you and, sooner or later, become a client of yours.

When I published by first book, *Levels UP*, there were people I had been promoting to and showering with useful content for several months, with the help of remarketing and email marketing, and then many of them bought the book. I sold many times more books through my site than all the bookstores did. I had announced all those bookstores on my webpage, and still I sold more.

Everything is a matter of good communication.

If you are wondering what remarketing is, I'll explain the basics.

Remarketing is continuous communication with a consumer through a variety of communication channels. Digital marketing provides you with this opportunity at a very reasonable price.

Imagine that the target audience of your product are 500,000 Bulgarian consumers. You decide to do a TV ad, which will cost you quite a lot. That's an effective and perhaps the most popular way for promoting widely-used products targeted at mass consumers.

But if you want to continue communicating with those who have seen your brand and come in contact with your business, but you don't have the budget necessary for TV advertising, you can achieve wonderful results through remarketing and dynamic remarketing.

Perhaps you'd like to know the difference between regular and dynamic remarketing, but you can check it up on the Internet. There's plenty of information on the subject. In short, when a consumer visits your site and browses some products without buying anything, through dynamic remarketing you may transform these products into ads that will haunt said consumer for a certain period of time. You determine this period, because the life of every audience is up to you. There is a maximum period, but it is rather long – in my opinion, needlessly so.

TV advertising is powerful, and it's still the most effective channel, but the Internet shouldn't be underestimated, especially if you cannot afford a TV presence. I already mentioned more than once that we live in a time of advertisement blindness, and if you are unable to retain interest in your brand and keep in contact with consumers, one TV advertising campaign may be even less effective that a year-round Internet presence.

On the other hand, your online presence can be easily combined with all other communication channels.

You see, whatever you do, you'll achieve more with excellent communication and a well-planned strategy. Many people aim at quantity and don't pay enough attention to quality. They prefer paying a few thousand and sending hundreds of thousands unsolicited messages (SPAM), instead of coming up with a strategy, compiling their own mailing lists, and communicating effectively with their potential customers. Of course, doing all this professionally takes more time, but the results justify all effort invested. Everyone running a business should try to do right by their customers, and not treat them in a way they don't want to be treated themselves.

Satisfied and well cared-for customers are a source of new ones!

But let us set digital marketing and audience management aside, and get back to persuasive communication and manipulation.

MANIPULATION AND DECEIT

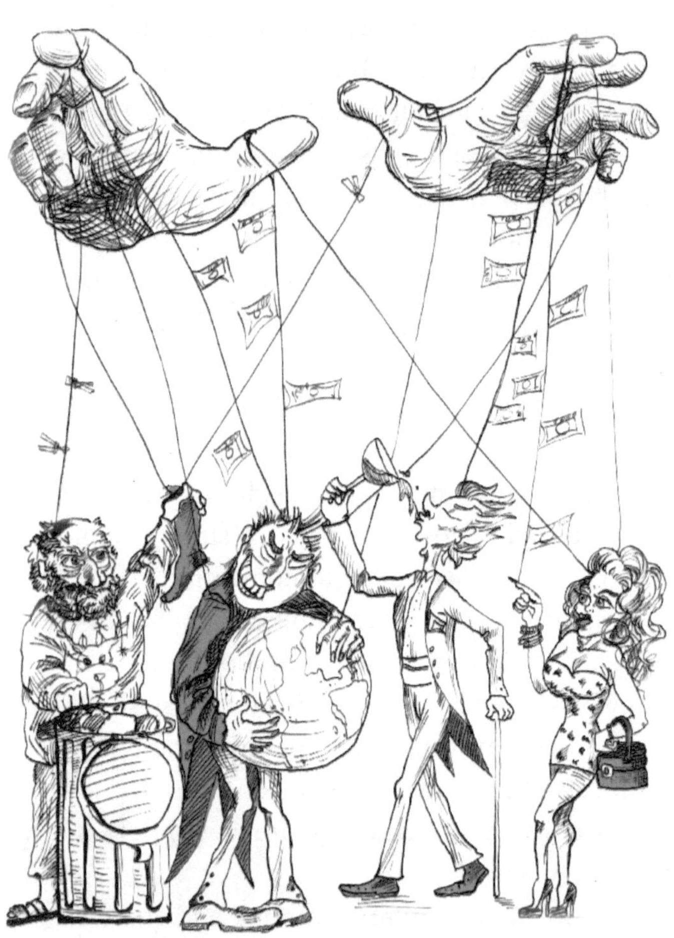

MANIPULATION

Every day we're swamped by advertisements that engender particular needs and control our purchases; everywhere we run into special offers and promoters. We're stressed, listening to news that breed fear. We fear for our future. For our children' future. We vaccinate. We follow every step that is said to be crucial for our safety. We are constantly being manipulated. We allow ourselves to fall prey to manipulation techniques. We believe we are doing what is right, we are trusting. Well-meaning.

But the world has changed. People study psychology and manipulation to become successful managers and leaders. Others learn demotivation and depersonalization in order to work for governments or other organizations that will use their skills for inhumane purposes. And you have to know how to protect yourself. Just like you've secured your home against thieves, you must secure the knowledge necessary to protect you against

manipulation and deceit.

On the other hand, if you'd like to run a business and motivate your employees, if you'd like to be a successful salesperson and broker lots of deals, you must know people and be able to tell them what they want to hear. You must be skillful at manipulating and stimulating them, master the art of deceit and be capable of playing various roles. It sounds scary, but it's true.

I don't recommend cheating and dishonesty; just the opposite, I've always been all for honest business, paid taxes and peaceful sleep. I've passed more than one opportunity for serious profit out of shady deals and schemes. And I don't regret any of them, because my conscience is clear, albeit unworthy of heaven.

Manipulation and motivation often go hand in hand. You may use these skills not to harm people, but to stimulate them and help them achieve great success, as well as business superiority.

You don't have a nice job because you don't have the necessary education. You can't get a better paid job because you don't have the required practice and work experience. Then you grow too old and they tell you young people have more energy than you, so yet again, you are not suitable for your dream job. And in the end, you don't have a good pension because you don't have enough years of service. That's our world today. People are being used and manipulated.

But you don't need to be one of them. Mastering the art of deceit and manipulation is crucial for your future success. But never forget that power struggles have no rules, and most people would invest more effort in bringing you down in achieving success themselves.

Most people are like open books: whatever's in their heart spills out of their mouth. They blurt out their opinions without thinking, and don't conceal their plans, even feel the need to share and discuss them. They believe they should be honest and sincere, as this would endear them to those around them. Unfortunately, such people are often bitterly disappointed. It's much wiser to carefully consider what you are about to say, and tell others only what they want or need to hear. It's important to avoid topics that will make you predictable and boring. If you have set your sights on success and leadership, forget selfless honesty and naked truths. But don't think it would be easy to disguise your intentions so that nobody suspects you.

DECEIT

Alex was an ambitious girl from a small town that didn't promise a particularly bright future to its inhabitants. That's why, she'd put a lot of effort in finding a job in the capital, and was willing to do anything to get away from poverty and routine.

And so came the day when she was hired by a huge Sofia company, and was now working hard under Sylvia in the Marketing department.

Alex looked humble, dressed modestly and did everything Sylvia and her colleagues asked her to. At first glance, she evoked pity; some people even made fun of her. They considered her awkward and old fashioned, and believed they could treat her almost like a servant. They had no idea about her excellent manipulation skills and great hunger for power.

Sylvia was a skilled manager and had the respect of all her colleagues and of the company executives, too. She didn't tolerate willfulness; any demonstration of disrespect ended in a penalty, or in rear cases even in dismissal. Most of her employees deemed her ruthless, others believed her fair. That was her weapon, helping her cling to power, and nobody could even imagine another taking her place. Not until she herself decided to work elsewhere.

Alex publicly admired her; for her, Sylvia was perfection personified, a valuable mentor and a wonderful manager. Alex expertly and slyly played her cards, as if she had perfected devising complex games while striving for power in a faraway kingdom. She looked weak and vulnerable in her alleged shying away from power, but was in fact totally different. She was keenly aware that to do battle, you needed a sharp sword and a strong shield. So, having armed herself with massive patience, she managed to deal with all the mockery and endless tasks. Her sharpened sword was deceit, and she was soon going to yield it with great expertise. While most of her coworkers spent years mastering different skills and enjoyed themselves in their free time, Alex was busy studying people's behavior, and would spend her spare hours communicating on Internet forums, dating sites and face to face. She was constantly drawing up personality profiles and improving her manipulation techniques. All this made her an excellent psychologist, and she actually knew about her colleagues much more than they knew about themselves.

At every lunch, party or teambuilding activity, Alex approached Sylvia. She knew Sylvia was a domineering woman and it would be easy to induce her to look after and protect poor Alex. Not long after, Alex was promoted. She was now Sylvia's right hand, taken under Sylvia's wing, and no one else ordered her around and assigned her tasks. Alex had learned the language of her patron. She said only what Sylvia wanted to hear, and here words were like balm for the manager's soul. And after Alex' tipping the scales more than once, many new faces joined the team and she decided it was time to set her sights on the highest target: replacing Sylvia as head of the department.

"Whatever mankind desires, that it will hope for and believe in."

—Adolf Hitler

Alex secured Sylvia's trust, and even made her dependent. The girl was so lavish in her praise and adoration that Sylvia was more assured than ever in her flawless appearance. Alex led her to believe she was the most stylish and desirable female in the office, making Sylvia act even more haughtily and overconfidently than before – which didn't go unnoticed by the company's executives. Sylvia was convinced she was irreplaceable, and the most successful manager this company had ever employed. Alex now had several ideas how to overthrow Sylvia, but she needed to make sure that she herself would be the one to take her place, and no one else. So Alex started complaining that nobody ever appreciated her, both in life and at work, and that if it wasn't for Sylvia, she may even have ended her life. Thus she made Sylvia into her guardian angel, melting the other woman's cold heart and making her do her best to change the situation. At every opportunity, Sylvia started praising Alex to the executives; she kept saying how diligent, creative and responsible Alex was. She even claimed Alex was the HR department's most valuable find. Unintentionally, Sylvia was paving the way for her replacement.

One day, Sylvia came to the office annoyed after being scolded by the directors. Alex had been waiting for such an opportunity for months, and offered Sylvia to go for a drink and a chat after work, not failing to mention that

Sylvia's superiors were unable to appreciate her dedication and professionalism.

That night, simply dressed Alex was sitting next to stunning Sylvia, dazzling in her expensive dress and stylish jewelry. It was a nice bar, pretty crowded but not too noisy, allowing them to talk. They ordered drinks and Alex, seemingly worried, asked Sylvia details about what had happened. Sylvia couldn't hide her rage and confided in Alex that she had not only been scolded, but also fined for her frequent late arrivals in the morning. For a time, Sylvia had felt like she owned the company, but today the executives had burst her bubble, and she didn't like it one bit.

While they were finishing the second bottle of wine, Alex timidly asked, "Sylvie, what's our advertisement budget?"

"Perhaps a million euros. Why do you ask, Alex?"

"Honey, don't you think our partners charge us too steeply? I know of companies that could offer us prices at least 30% lower."

"Mind your own business, Alex. That's my job. I won't deal with incompetent little firms. We'd better pay more but receive a high quality service."

"Sylvie, I think you work too hard and get too little in return. I can't fathom how they could make such a big deal of a few late mornings, and humiliate you with their fines, when you're so dedicated to their business!"

That was exactly what Sylvia needed to hear. Slightly tipsy, she hugged Alex and burst into tears on her shoulder.

At this moment of weakness, Alex said sharply, "I have a plan. I know you won't agree and will say you know better, as always, but please listen first." Sylvia nodded, and Alex went on. "I know we have two main advertisement partners that we use most. The bosses are happy with them, but they charge dearly. The company is already experiencing difficulties, they've let thirty seven people go over the last few months."

Sylvia stared, wide-eyed, and nodded in bewilderment.

"If you tell the big bosses you could cut our marketing costs down by no less than 15-20% by replacing our partner agencies with smaller, but reliable companies which would give an arm and a leg to work with us, you'd make them happy yet again. Of course, you'd tell them you are ready to take the risk, which will be a burden for me and the department, but it is a sacrifice for the company you are willing to make."

Sylvia laughed and patted Alex. "Honey, that won't be much of an improvement. It would indeed free some capital, but the burden would be too great, and I doubt it anybody would appreciate it for long. I'd rather not do it."

Then Alex looked Sylvia right in the eye and said, "What if the other 10% are for us?"

Sylvia reacted harshly. "What are you blabbering about? Have you lost your mind? And be quiet, someone may hear this nonsense! Or are you drunk?"

Alex shook her head and continued. "Sylvie, in a year or two, you'll fall out with the bosses, they'll give our jobs to others, and then what? Has it all been for nothing? Don't you see that even now, when you do your best, when you're so strong and motivated – they still don't appreciate you? In time, things will only get worse. Don't you think we can use an additional hundred thousand a year?"

This was too much for Sylvia. She gulped another glass of wine almost in one go, while Alex kept talking. "Look, honey, we'll find new partners and work with them only if they offer us better prices and agree to give us a commission of 10%. We'll put up a shell company and issue an invoice for these 10%, so that everything adds up accounting-wise. Anybody would want to bag assignments worth hundreds of thousands; all small agencies crave clients like us, so they'll be willing to do whatever we want. And they won't betray us because that would mean losing a client, get it?"

Sylvia could only stare, stunned; the whole conversation came like a bolt from the blue. Tonight she saw Alex in a totally different light. The whole scheme, on top of the alcohol, befuddled her entirely, and she didn't know what to say. She excused herself, saying she was not feeling well, and called a taxi. She thought they had drunk too much and were not speaking seriously. The taxi came and Sylvia left, thoughtful and somewhat troubled. That's what Alex counted upon: if her idea got rejected, she could use the alcohol as an excuse. But she was sure Sylvia would give it some serious thought.

The next day, the two friends worked slightly hungover, and exchanged guilty glances as if they'd committed a crime. Shortly before they had to go home, Sylvia asked Alex if she had time for a drink and a talk after work. Only an hour later, they were ordering drinks at the same bar they had visited the previous night.

"Alex, were you serious last night?"

Alex feigned extreme concern. "Yes, Sylvie, I'm tired of seeing you give your all for nothing. I see how much effort you put in, and I believe you deserve more."

Sylvia nodded and asked what exactly Alex had in mind. Alex had come prepared, and explained the whole scheme in detail. Sylvia promised to think about it, but in fact she had already made up her mind, and Alex knew it. In a month, they had already set up a shell company and were negotiating with new partners. After they agreed on good prices, 10% commission and complete confidentiality, Sylvia asked to meet with the executives and present her idea for cutting down expenses without changing the company's marketing strategy. Together with her right hand Alex, Sylvia prepared an impressive and persuasive presentation, which was met with satisfaction and agreement. Sylvia was praised an encouraged to act, and the very next day she gave an assignment to her new partners. The two friends started earning a lot on the side, but cleverly concealed their income.

Alex was very pleased with herself, and decided not to go through with her plan to overthrow Sylvia. Instead of taking Sylvia's place, Alex decided to fight for an equal cut; at the time, Sylvia took 70% of their extracurricular income to Alex' 30%.

Again drinking at the bar, Alex asked Sylvia for an equal share. "Honey, why don't we split 50/50? I work just as hard as you and risk as much."

At that moment, Sylvia decided she couldn't refuse Alex' request because she had seen what the young woman could do. She agreed without arguing, and proposed a toast for their new profitable enterprise. Alex was very pleased; in fact, she took a much smaller risk, because she could always deny everything, and after all, Sylvia was head of the department.

Perhaps you're wondering what happened next? It doesn't matter. What matters is to learn from this story. Everybody knows that smart people learn not only from their own mistakes, but also from those of others.

Power is an extraordinary game, because the whole of society is involved. To learn its rules and subtleties, you should study its art diligently, should understand human desires and peculiarities. You should recognize the hidden reasons that drive those around you to a certain decision, not letting the fog they cover their true motivation with confuse you. People are extremely complex creatures, and you could waste a huge portion of your life trying to study them without managing to understand them completely. That's why it's in your best interests to start training in this art as soon as possible.

So now it's time for the most important chapter in this book: "Reading the signs". It's a clever skill that many people believe they possess, allowing them not to miss anything in a conversation.

READING THE **SIGNS**

Time flies so fast; could it have been twenty years since I started my first business? Over that time, I've made a great effort to study people and test different sales strategies. I've analyzed thousands of meetings, most of which I recorded on my portable tape recorder and then played in the evenings, trying to spot my mistakes. It was a lot of work, a lot of tension, but on the other hand, I've lived an extremely interesting and amusing life. I don't regret a thing, and although now I spend my days training salespeople and sales teams, I keep learning and analyzing. It has all become a necessity, and I don't think I'd be able to stop. Thus, over the years, I realized how many things we miss during a conversation. In our rush to talk, we forget to ask questions that may help us read the signs.

I discovered the power of active listening, of teamwork, motivation, smiles, good manners, intellect and wit, self-confidence, aromas, resolve and gestures. My practice as a business coach helped me ask the relevant questions, provoking the other to talk and hand me clues that I could use and reuse in the conversation, helping this person to unlock their potential and achieve goals that they haven't even dreamt of setting themselves. I call this skill I discovered "reading the signs". To uncover all the signs in a conversation is not easy, it requires good concentration and a sharp mind, so that you can put them to good use as soon as you spot them.

SELLING A BLOOD PRESSURE MONITOR

Here's a scenario. Maria is a consultant pharmacist serving Mrs. Petrova, who intends to purchase a new blood pressure monitor. Mrs. Petrova wishes to buy the cheapest mechanical model, while **Maria's task is to sell a digital device, which is three times as expensive as the mechanical one**. The question is, will Maria be able to read the signs in this conversation? And will you?

Since the beginning of this book I've been telling you stories, focusing primarily on signs and clues. I hope you'll manage to discover the ones in this sales scenario and the others that follow, and come up with ways of using them even before you've read about it.

Mrs. Petrova came in the pharmacy and headed for the blood pressure monitors display. That section was assigned to Maria, a young consultant pharmacist.

"Hello", said Mrs. Petrova.

"Hello, how can I help you?"

"Can you show me the cheapest blood pressure monitor?"

"Here, this is the cheapest one." Maria reached for one of the cheapest mechanical monitors and handed it to Mrs. Petrova.

"Excuse me, can you tell me how much it is? I can't read the price."

"Sure, madam, this monitor costs 19.50 leva."

"Is it good? Does it have a warranty period?"

"Yes, it's a decent monitor, two years of warranty. We have other models as well, some of them digital. They are very good and many people prefer them, but they are more expensive."

"How much is a digital one?"

"85 leva. But it's extremely accurate."

"Isn't the mechanical one accurate as well?"

"It is, but some people find it harder to use, so they prefer the digital one."

"I won't have any difficulties. I've been taking my blood pressure daily and I'm used to it. I'll take the mechanical one."

Did you notice the clue in this conversation? What was Maria's mistake? Here, there was a very easy-to-spot sign, which could have been used right away to tip the scales in favor of the digital monitor. When Mrs. Petrova asked Maria to read her the price, it was our first clue: **"I can't see well."** Maria made one more mistake: she said that many people prefer the digital monitor, but it was more expensive. We should never label our products as "expensive". Each one has its quality, and a price to go with it.

Let's see how the conversation might have gone if Maria had read the signs.

"Hello", said Mrs. Petrova.

"Hello, how can I help you?"

"Can you show me the cheapest blood pressure monitor?"

"Here, this is the cheapest one." Maria reached for one of the cheapest mechanical monitors and handed it to Mrs. Petrova.

"Excuse me, **can you tell me how much it is? I can't read the price**."

"Sure, madam, this monitor costs 19.50 leva. Are your eyes bothering you as well?"

"Yes, besides the high blood pressure, I have glaucoma, perhaps it's related. Is this monitor good? Does it have a warranty period?"

"You said you have glaucoma. That can cause headaches. While trying to take your blood pressure, did you sometimes keep hearing your pulse too loudly, preventing you from reading your blood pressure correctly?"

"Yes, it happens quite often."

"Then I have a better offer for you, madam. Look at this monitor, it has a large display and you don't have to be quiet and concentrated to hear your pulse and take your blood pressure. You will be able to see the reading quite easily. You just have to put it on your arm and press this button, and in seconds your blood pressure values will appear on the screen. It takes your pulse as well."

"And how much does this digital monitor cost?"

"It's a very good price, 85 leva."

"That's quite expensive."

"It's a top-notch blood pressure monitor. It's up to you, but I think your health must come first. It's not by chance that this monitor has a five-year warranty. The mechanical one is okay, but in your situation, isn't it better to have a digital one at hand?"

"You are right, I'll take the digital one."

Reading the signs correctly doesn't guarantee closing the deal, but it definitely improves your chances. It triggers asking additional questions, which can lead to more clues, like in this case. Thanks to the first clue, we uncovered another one – "I have glaucoma". Weakened eyesight and glaucoma helped strengthen Maria's argument, and she sold the digital monitor with ease.

It's a great idea to hold such deal simulations among your sales reps; they help improve creativity and sharpness of mind. Companies usually train only with products from their own portfolio, and primarily organize product training sessions so that their employees get to know what they are selling. This is very important, but it's definitely not enough, since it doesn't hone the consultants' sales skills.

SELLING A HIGH-END MATTRESS

As in the previous example, try to notice the signs and the other mistakes in the conversation before reading about them.

Nevena worked as a consultant in a huge furniture store and was assigned the Bedroom sector. Her task was to sell Mr. Ignatov a more high-end, more expensive mattress than the one he had his eyes on.

"Hello, I have a question about a mattress." Mr. Ignatov said to the charming consultant.

"Sure, how can I help you?"

"I was wondering, how much would this one here cost, if it were queen sized?"

"Sure, let me see. 380 leva. It's a traditional spring mattress, double-sided. Here you can see a cross-section picture. It's seven inches thick."

"Okay, I see you offer quite the selection of mattresses, which one would you recommend?"

"Well, what's your budget? Prices vary in a very wide range, we have mattresses up to 3000 leva. These here are better, high-end, but they cost 900 leva or more."

"Well, I cannot spare more than 500-600 leva."

"Unfortunately, this price range cannot offer much more. All high-end mattresses are much more expensive."

"Why are they better than the one I picked? Is it low quality?"

"No, it's very good for a spring mattress."

"I've seen ads, they say spring mattresses are the only real mattresses."

"Forget the ads, have a look at these here. That's a high-end mattress with memory foam. When you lie down, it takes the shape of your body, and then restores its original shape after you get up. It provides extreme comfort and guarantees good sleep. Why don't you lie on one of the mattresses to try it? You can see for yourself how comfortable it is."

"Okay, which one should I try out?"

"This one here."

"Yes, it really feels very soft and nice."

"Now come try another one, it's a bit harder than the first."

"Okay. Yes, this one is also very comfortable, maybe even more so than the first. I'll have to think about it. Thank you very much, have a nice day!"

"You too."

That's how you lose a client. Surefire clients are often lost due to the consultants' attempts at wittiness or their lack of knowledge on how to communicate and what questions to ask. Constant talking keeps you from noticing the signs. Clients often don't give away any if you don't provoke them with your questions.

In the example above, Nevena didn't ask a single relevant question that could help her gather valuable information.

Let's see if asking questions could have uncovered some clues and changed the situation.

"Hello, I have a question about a mattress." Mr. Ignatov said to the charming consultant.

"Sure, how can I help you?"

"I was wondering, how much would this one here cost, if it were queen sized?"

"Sure, I'll check right away. But first, please tell me, will *you* be using the mattress?"

"No, my daughter married and they're now moving to their own place. My wife and I would like to buy a mattress for their new bed."

"How wonderful! I assume you'd like to buy a nice mattress that doesn't squeak and is very comfortable. The mattress shouldn't be a cause for quarrels in the new family."

"Yes, absolutely."

"I suggest we skip these mattresses here, in time they begin to squeak, and it gets rather loud when … you know." Nevena pretended to feel awkward and Mr. Ignatov blushed slightly. But after all, this was something natural and had to be taken into account when purchasing a mattress for newlyweds that would presumably lead an active sex life.

"I haven't thought about that, to be honest."

"No problem, that's why I'm here, to help you choose the best mattress. Tell me, do your daughter or her husband have any aches?"

"No, she's a gymnast, and he's very healthy too, he owns a car repairs shop."

"Oh, if she's a gymnast, she must be rather slim?"

"Very, she seems almost fragile next to him."

"So he's a large man?"

"Exactly so."

"You've given me very useful information, and I can offer you two alternatives to choose from. Since she's slim and he's burly, they probably won't feel comfortable on a mattress with equally firm surface. If you take medium hard, it will be too soft for him because he's heavy. If you take hard, it will be too hard for her. So you have two options, either buying two mattresses that they can place on their bed side by side, or even better, a dual-core mattress. One half harder for him, and the other softer for her."

"Gosh, I didn't even know such things were possible. I've never thought about those details. Will a budget of 600 leva be enough?"

"Absolutely not, but if you go with the first option, I can make you a great offer for a little more: for 900 leva, you'll be making a great gift and then some. The first option does not require a special order, we have suitable mattresses on hand, so you could buy them, let the couple sleep on them for a week or two, and then, if they are not happy, we could replace them."

"Sounds great, let's do it."

Questions require answers, and answers often contain clues. The conversation can go in many different directions, the outcome not always being a deal, but you must learn how to be an active listener and ask the right questions. You shouldn't talk and demonstrate competence before reading the signs. Did you see how a single question – "Will *you* be using it?" – opened up the conversation. It is a relevant question, because if the client himself were to use the mattress, it would have been best for him to lie on it and try it out. If it was for him, the questions that followed would have focused on him.

He could have been buying mattresses for a hotel or a new apartment. If so, he may have needed children's mattresses as well, so we could have offered some. Then we could have made a package deal, increasing the amount spent considerably.

We should never offer only what the client is looking for. We should discreetly ask relevant questions to help us know more. We should also come up with a strategy that shifts the focus from the price towards the added value we bring to the value exchange, i.e. the sale. In the example above, right after telling the client he had to rethink his budget, the salesperson shifted the focus to the two options. It's a good strategy to offer the client a limited choice, making him focus on the options and not on overspending his budget. Why should he think of the price when he has two options, and they are both over budget? Of course, each specific situation defines the strategy, and a dealer should be flexible enough to assess the situation, and not put off a client by making too steep an offer.

EXPANDING ON THE SALE

In the example below, thanks to reading the signs correctly, Iliana will expand on the sale and increase its value dramatically.

Follow the conversation closely and again try to notice the clues before reading about them, and guess how Iliana could use them to expand on the sale.

Iliana was a consultant in a store offering luxury tobacco products and a special selection of high-end wines. She always engaged clients in such a way as to provoke them to tell her more and feed her clues that she could very expertly use. She was an excellent saleswoman and her great results were bound to get her noticed.

Stanley entered the store and headed straight for the cigars. Before Iliana could offer him her help, he said, "Hello, I'll be having guests from England and I'd like to buy some good cigars for the guys. It'll be a nice surprise for them."

Few people have minds sharp enough to instantly supply them with questions and different scenarios for improving the sale; few notice every clue, and even if they do, they don't always use it correctly. You know from playing cards that a strong first hand don't always guarantee victory; the same is valid for sales and clues.

Even after uncovering them, if you don't use them correctly, you'll be wasting them and won't be closing the deal in the way you want.

In the example above, we already have a clue, and if you think it's the fact that Stanley is having guests from England, you are wrong. What Stanley gives away is that he's buying cigars *for the guys*, which means that there will probably be women present as well. Let's see how this clue will help Iliana and how she's going to play her cards now.

"I'll help you find the best cigars for the evening, but you said guys, will there be girls as well?"

"Yes, there will be."

"Do they smoke?"

"Oh, I don't think so, but even if they do, I've planned a guys night and a game of poker, no women involved. They'll be doing something else."

"You know, in order to have a nice night with your friends, won't it be better to mollify the women with some excellent wine? You are probably aware that we offer great wine selections here. How many female guests are you expecting, actually?"

"Four will be coming, so my wife makes five."

"In that case, my advice is to buy white wine and rosé. Thus you'll cater for every taste. What do you say? You know, we women love to drink wine and share girly stuff."

"Yes, it seems like a good idea to buy wine for the girls, but perhaps I should buy some white only."

"You could, but if you'd really like to impress the girls as well as the guys, they'd better have a choice. Many women prefer rosé, but the white is still the most popular choice at that time of year.”

“Okay, let’s pick some cigars, and then I’ll buy wine for the women. It’s no secret that if they aren’t happy, we won’t be either.” Stanley laughed and listened with interest to Iliana’s stories about the different types of cigars.

A single phrase, and still such an important clue – “for the guys”. One successfully uncovered clue becomes the basis for a pleasant conversation, it brings about emotions, jokes and high spirits. And once there’s pleasant emotions and a good mood, both selling and expanding on the sale get easier.

The examples I’ve described, in different variations, have been played out at numerous trainings and, to be honest, few salespeople have managed to read the signs, even knowing that’s the purpose of the exercise. It’s even harder in a neutral setting, during a spontaneous conversation. To master this skill, you need practice. Recording your conversations and analyzing them can be very useful, because when you see or hear yourself from the outside, you spot and take in lots of oversights and opportunities which you haven’t noticed during the conversation itself.

Many years ago, in 2007, I had the pleasure of working with an excellent mentor. He recorded everything so that he could return to any meeting at any time. He was a very successful businessman and not so great a salesman, but I definitely appreciated his habits and strict discipline in managing contacts and clients’ files. Then I wondered whether it was worth doing the same with all my meetings. And it led to a great breakthrough in my professional development. My analyses got more and more interesting, because I started seeing the many mistakes I've made, and gradually I became aware of many clues that have been lying around but I've failed to notice and use. Truth be told, despite my extensive practice in sales, it was then that my real growth in negotiating and profile building started.

That's why I said that long practice in the field is not enough to make you a real salesperson. A series of actions, no matter how many times you repeat them, achieve the same results every time. If you never change the way you hit the ball, it will always follow the same imperfect curve you wish to avoid.

Sales require constant work and analyzing, as well as honing your skills in active listening, asking the right questions, letting go of aggression and mastering your ego.

Every time I go for a walk, I notice mistakes: mistakes in store windows, mistakes in brochures – but not spelling mistakes, conceptual ones. Okay, perhaps it's a professional deformation, but I don't like seeing a company blow serious money on the wrong thing. And even if I told them it were wrong, it would be useless, because in marketing, it's not like 2+2=4, there are constant disputes what works and what doesn't. The way things should be done, of course, is a matter of opinion. On the other hand though, marketing is based on undeniable and smoothly running principles which few marketing and advertisement experts are aware of.

One day, while my children were playing in the kid zone at one of the city malls, I went for a walk and felt drawn to the huge window of an optical store. The store was over 1000 square feet, and the window alone was over 30 feet long and 9 feet high. And in the most visible spot, at the very front, they had put up a poster that explained in detail what their newest offer included: which types of glasses it covered, and all the other specifics. So 65 square feet now looked something like the Terms and Conditions page on a website. And the offer was actually quite appealing.

When you pay serious rent, have a lot of staff and decide to do a special offer, you should also have a strategy.

People didn't need to have all the information before even entering the store. By doing so, the owners had turned the front into a book page, and people didn't pay it any attention. There was too much text, so nobody bothered to read it and learn about the good offer.

Build your messages around certain key principles, such as:

» Attention: decorate the window in such a way that it grabs the attention

» Interest: it should arouse people's interest and curiosity, making them come into the store

» Appeal: once in the store, consumers should be stimulated by the staff to buy, hearing about all the options and conditions of the offer

» Action: in the end, there should be a deal or whatever the desired outcome is.

We can't let the chips fall as they may; we must have a communication strategy and interact with consumers strategically, in a creative instead of an aggressive way.

But let's go back to the ability of reading the signs. I'll give you a few more examples to assist you with mastering persuasive communication and effective sales.

SELLING A LAWN MOWER

Milena was a consultant in the Garden department of a huge store specializing in home and garden equipment. In the lawn mower zone, Beatrice was trying to find a suitable, noiseless mower for her family's yard.

"Hello, madam, can I help you?" asked Milena.

Beatrice smiled. "Hello, I can definitely use some help. I don't see the difference between these mowers, I'd like to buy a high-end electric one."

Milena hardly waited for Beatrice to finish, plunging into an explanation about how much more convenient petrol lawn mowers were in comparison to electric ones. "Madam, electric models are corded, and the cable can always entangle in something or you may not notice it and run it over, which will be pretty bad."

In ten minutes, Milena had listed all the advantages of petrol lawn mowers, and the respective disadvantages of electric ones. It turned out that their only saving grace was the lower price, but Beatrice was definitely not looking for a cheaper model.

Milena forgot to ask questions, failed to inquire how large Beatrice's yard was, how she had taken care of the grass up to this point, whether she had ever used a mower, and many other things that could have helped her serve a client with a conscious need. Instead, her abundant knowledge of the technical side and her lack of sales skills put her at a disadvantage, driving the client back.

"You know, I really appreciate all this information, you spared me from making a mistake. I have an excellent petrol mower, but it's too noisy, and my kids are still young. On top of that, if someone mows the lawn while we're outside by the pool, the smell of exhaust fumes drives me mad. But I haven't thought about the cord and the other drawbacks. I really don't want the electricity harming somebody. I changed my mind, I won't buy another mower. Have a nice day!"

Milena hurried to explain that the mower had safeguards so nobody would come to harm, but it only made things worse. You can't lax lyrical about a machine's poor quality, and then start praising it. One relevant question at the start, and everything would have gone quite differently. Perhaps, if she had the patience to listen to Beatrice without interrupting, she would have even learned that Beatrice already had a petrol mower. But Milena's rush to talk and consult prevented her from closing the deal, as this is very often the case: no clues uncovered, no sale.

SELLING A JACKET

Steve was an athlete, tall and well-built, and Monny was a consultant in a fancy store for male clothing. As soon as he went through the door, Steve was heartily welcomed by Monny. He was immediately offered assistance so that he could make the best choice. Monny hurried to cater to all of Steve's needs, and so eventually, Steve tried on a jacket that fit him perfectly and was obviously to his liking.

"You look great, sir, this cut is exactly for people like you. The jacket is close fitting and it's not suitable for shorter people or plump ones, but on you, it hangs perfectly."

That was the honest truth, so Monny didn't lie to the customer. But failing to ask the relevant questions, he didn't know that Steve was actually looking for a jacket not for himself, but for his brother, a lawyer, who was shorter than him and working at a desk, which had a disastrous effect on his waist.

"I see. That's very useful to know, because I'm buying a jacket for my brother. He's shorter and on the plump side, which means this one here won't fit him. Which model would be right for him?"

At this point, Monny regretted his words, because the jacket Steve had on was in fact the least fitted; all the other models had an even closer fit, making them unsuitable for Steve's brother. So Monny tried to be sly and sell a gift certificate instead. "You know, sir, you'd better buy a gift certificate for your brother, so he can come in person. Once he picks a model, we can even tailor it so that it feels more comfortable and looks good on him. Each body is different."

"You are right, but at least show me some loosely fitting models so that I can see if you have something suitable."

"Actually, the jacket you tried on is the least fitting."

"Then I think I'll have to look elsewhere. I appreciate your advice about the certificate, I'll buy one from the store I choose. Have a nice day."

"You too, sir."

Monny's haste to convince Steve that the jacket was right for him, as well as his failure to inquire if Steve was actually buying a jacket for himself, caused the client to leave the store despite his preference for the brand.

A single relevant question, and Monny would have had a clue and sold a gift certificate with no trouble at all. But his desire to talk lost him the deal. Of course, that's not the only problem; an even greater loss is that he failed to learn anything about Steve. He didn't know if he was a regular client of the brand. That's an easy mistake to make: salespersons not collecting data about potential customers.

You should always have a strategy how to collect data out of everyone, or almost everyone, coming in contact with your business.

In the example above, Monny could have asked Steve whether he had a loyalty card – this would have made it clear if he was a regular customer or not. You can't just inquire out of the blue, "Hello, are you a client of ours?"; it would be out of place.

If it turned out that Steve was not a client, he may have been offered a short survey to pinpoint his interests in men's clothing, so that he could receive email notifications about new collections and discounts only on those articles he was interested in.

You can't let people just walk out of the door and forget about your business. Every visit is worth money, and such an attitude and the lack of communication strategy will directly affect the profits of a business. Everything is a form of communication, and even meeting the client right at the door is poor communication. You can't start interacting with them as soon as they cross the threshold. You should know that if it's a small store, the client doesn't feel properly inside until they've made it at least 9 feet in; in a large store, the distance is even greater. The lack of adequate communication may cause the loss of many customers, and lead to lots of missed opportunities, so you must improve your own communication skills and those of your employees.

PRICE IS NOT ALL THERE IS

People are often under the impression that price is all, and the rest hardly matters. They highly underestimate marketing and the power of effective communication with customers. They believe that once they have secured the lowest price, that's their best communicative advantage, and it's more than enough to make them number one – but that's hardly the case. I'll give you a very simplified example.

How did the word "simplified" make you feel? You shouldn't tell people you'll be giving them "simplified" examples. It's like telling someone, "You'll hardly understand me otherwise, so let me put it very simple." It would be like telling them your explanation is for simpletons. Every word counts, so you must learn to use the correct ones that will show you to the best advantage.

Actually, I really intended to give you an example of why price is not everything.

A market stall sells wonderful ripe tomatoes. They are beautifully arranged and cost 2 leva, but the seller doesn't let his clients pick the ones they want. He chooses for them from the produce in the crates next to him, so that they don't ruin the nicely arranged display.

The next stall also sells tomatoes. It's not well arranged at all, but the price is 1.70 leva. Unfortunately, this seller also doesn't allow customers to pick their own tomatoes, because they can squash them and many will go to waste.

A third stall also offers nice ripe tomatoes. It is not arranged very well and doesn't appeal so much as the first one, but here there is a sign "You can pick what you like", and the price is 2.30. This stall is preferred by all and sells the most tomatoes. Sure, more produce probably goes to waste than at the other stalls, but it's still the best strategy, because the price difference of 0.30-0.50 per pound allows the trader for 1 pound of waste to every 8 to 10 pounds of sold tomatoes. Meanwhile, he's giving his customers what's most valuable of all: the opportunity to pick for themselves. Yet again, better communication and marketing strategy beat lower prices.

And imagine, if you could have both reasonable prices and excellent communication – your competitors could only dream of your results.

I know that, despite everything I said, many of you still think price is what matters most, and the possibility of offering the lowest price is a great advantage. But again, it depends primarily on the business in question.

While some companies try to beat the competition by lowering prices, others influence people's thinking and make millions. It all depends on your strategy and the way you market and communicate your business and product.

Some time ago, the market was swamped by the Power Balance silicone wristbands. They were pretty ordinary bands, with a holographic image at the center, covered by a transparent film. At first, these bracelets sold for $100. They were said to enhance the body, reduce stress and what not, and were marketed as pretty much indispensable. And despite their shocking price, they sold very successfully. Luxury stalls at the malls offered them, just like offering expensive jewelry. The bands came in lavish packaging, and their owners were so happy you'd think they'd found peace and harmony for the first time.

The bracelet became trendy and made its creators very rich. It all happened while other companies tried, and are still trying, to sell all kinds of gadgets: designer electronic bracelets, bracelets that synchronize with your smartphone, fitness bracelets that take your pulse and blood pressure and calculate how many miles you've walked and how many calories you've burnt. None of those managed to overshadow the ordinary silicone band that people bought with a smile, obviously aware that it was probably worth no more than a dollar.

Of course, there are many other examples that clearly illustrate price is not what matters most. Let's take a look at Pet Rock. They sell rocks, you know – massive rocks to use as pets, for the humble price of $19.95 and free shipping.

Is their business flourishing? Pretty much. It's going stronger than that of other companies selling goods much more costly to produce, and at the same time having a lower selling price. It's just that Pet Rock solves a problem in a really intelligent way. The true sellers of their products are the parents.

Every child wants a pet, but that's a serious responsibility. If you buy your child a dog, you have to take it for walks, feed it, treat it when it's sick, take special care of it when it grows old, and eventually, sadly, bury it when it dies. You can spare yourself all this trouble if you convince your child how trendy it is to have a pet rock.

And when one child owns something trendy, all the other kids want it too. This time, their parents support them, because as the people behind Pet Rock say, it needs no feeding and no walking, and will live forever. So you have to think strategically; don't be influenced by what others say about price and competition.

I can give you many more examples to illustrate the power of reading the signs and persuasive communication even further, because I always use such examples in the daily trainings I've been doing. But I think you are now aware of what you have to do to improve your communication skills and those of your employees.

And now, before proceeding to the final part of the book, I'll tell you what your business, product or service needs most. It's called unique selling point – USP. By creating a USP for your business, product or service, that will definitely help you stand out, even if you don't offer the lowest price.

It's not necessary for the USP to be truly unique; it's enough that you're the first to offer it. In fact, you can turn ordinary features into USPs by declaring them unique.

Let me give you some examples. Imagine a bottle of correction fluid. You know those – a small bottle with a brush that looks a bit like nail polish remover, but is applied to documents to mask your errors.

Let's say that the fluid of a certain brand does not crumble after drying. Imagine buying a bottle and seeing it written on the label: "Does not crumble after drying". You'll immediately ask yourself: "Do other correction fluids crumble?" But even if you don't remember any of them doing so, you'd be safer buying the one that says it explicitly.

In a similar manner, in one of SEIKO's campaigns, they claim that their watches work even 300 feet underwater. Sounds incredible, doesn't it? But think about it: when was the last time you went 300 feet under? As a beginner, I am allowed 30 feet at the most, but as far as I know, the pressure at 300 feet would be a challenge even for experienced divers. But that's a great USP that distinguishes these watches, and after all, if a watch can work at 300 feet underwater, it's probably safe to take it in the shower.

A chain of stores released the following statement: "We guarantee you the lowest price; or we'll pay you back the difference." That's enough to leave customers with the impression that everything there is cheapest, or the store wouldn't offer to reimburse someone who found the product at a lower price elsewhere. But in fact, they offer to pay you only the difference. In other words, if you buy a yoghurt for 1 lev at this store, but find it in another for 0.95 and prove that with a receipt, you'll be paid the difference of 0.05 lv. You can imagine how few people would do that. In this way, the store doesn't always need to sell at the lowest prices, but people go there thinking they're in for a bargain. It's a great and very persuasive USP.

I can give you many more examples for unique selling points, or as some call them, unique selling propositions, but I think you already know what you need to do about your product and business.

Think how you can influence people's thinking, because good positioning is not about the product, but about getting into customers' heads.

Have you noticed what happens when you pass by a Greek bakery? If you've ever been near one, you must have sensed the overpowering smell of vanilla. It makes you want to go right in and buy some of the deliciously smelling, freshly baked goods. Truth is, the smell doesn't come from them, but out of the air fresheners which spray out the aroma of vanilla and almonds every five minutes. That's also a type of communication, just as merchandising is both communication and science.

It's one thing to pass by a bakery where you see burnt trays and unwashed windows, and smell something unidentifiable, but by no means pleasant. It's quite another to pass by a bakery that is enveloped in a wonderful smell, stimulating your senses. Yes, the owners of the second one have made an investment – and it pays well, don't you think?

Did you know that a single banner over the racks in a store can change the amount of products sold? The position of the cash desk and the route the customer takes after entering the store also matter. It matters which products are placed in immediate proximity, and a slight rearrangement immediately affects the amounts spent, and the sales of related products. But I'll leave the topic of proper business structure for my other book, *Business above the Red Line*, where you can find lots of useful information about price-formation and market positioning, as well as other helpful tips for running a business. If you find this book useful and believe it will help you with sales and persuasive communication, then *Business above the Red Line* will give you priceless advice about your current or future business.

Every day, I come across different problems in different companies, and help managers and their teams with business growth and building marketing and sales strategies. I also lead business trainings, but whatever issues I have to deal with, they almost always stem from the same thing. Some realize it, others don't, but nearly all of them have problems with communication – be it corporate, marketing, persuasive, related to after-sales services, etc. Yet this problem is often underestimated, and money is spent on much less important things.

Don't underrate the power of communication – it can take you places where the lowest price never could.

And before thanking you for your time, I'll share some valuable information on effective sales: the so-called golden rules of selling, even if they are not relevant to every single business.

ALWAYS START WITH **THE HIGHEST PRICE**

Here's what mean. Let's say you're selling products A, B and C. Whatever they cost, the end consumer will always find them expensive, regardless of which price bracket you are in; and if they are truly cheap, they'll be regarded with suspicion.

Let's say product A costs 30 leva, product B – 20 leva, product C – 10 leva, and they are complementary goods. They can be bought separately, but it's best to be purchased together; that's why they are offered as a set, priced 45 leva, which is a much better bargain than buying them individually. But if you simply group the products in a set and price it 45 leva, nobody will know it's a good bargain; even if it says so on the tag. People take things for granted and will assume that's the regular price.

Now imagine you have a client that can use all three products. It will be much more effective to present them one by one, citing the price of each. Thus, you'll arrive at a total of 60 leva; but luckily for the client, these products are also available as a set at a special price of 45 leva until the end of the week, or due to a clearance sale.

When presenting to clients, each new price has to be lower, not higher. If you start at the bottom and the client finds the price too high, each option that follows will only be getting worse. That's why it's a good strategy to present the above products at their regular prices and then announce the special offer. It's not the same as announcing the offer first and then mentioning the individual prices. On the surface it may look the same, but the second option is much less effective because you deviate from the established model, i.e. "always start with the highest price".

Let's say a client is interested in product X, and its price varies from 200 to 2000 leva. If you start by 200 leva and they don't like your suggestion, every offer that follows will grow more expensive. If you start with the highest price, even if the client finds it shocking, that won't be a problem, because you can offer alternatives at lower prices. Every offer that follows will be more manageable, but as you are well aware, top quality and low prices don't go together. Toward the lower end of the price range, the client starts realizing that it means serious decrease in quality, and now the 200 leva option seems too cheap. They'll be very likely to choose something mid-range, and even if they pick the cheapest option, their demands will have dropped on the way to the lowest price. It will be easy to cope with future objections and discontent, because the client has chosen a low-budget option despite being aware of the alternatives.

In the majority of cases, not to say in almost all of them, sellers assume what their client's financial situation is without knowing anything about them. They draw conclusions about the client's solvency only on the basis of appearance, which is highly unprofessional. For that very reason, they offer a product at a certain price, and if it doesn't appeal, the following offers grow more and more expensive, and so grow the client's demands, because we bring them up the ladder, and the way up is paved by various claims. If you put them on the highest rung right away, there's no rise or fall. We have a product of certain quality that costs a certain amount. By going in either direction, we affect the client's expectations and mood, so we should always do so to our advantage. If you start at 200 leva and reach 2000 leva, going through several options, the client will demand a product of impossible quality.

Don't be afraid to start at the top; you should know that selling cheap is the hardest!

Now I'll share with you yet another golden rule of sales: never tell the client that something is expensive, but it's worth the money. Or that another thing is even more costly. When a client claims your product is expensive, don't agree with them. Many sellers say, "Yes, it's expensive, but it's top quality." This way, you agree that the price is indeed high. You'd better reply with a suitable phrase or a question.

Here's some examples:

– We have a budget option, sir, let me show you.

– Aren't you worth it?

– Don't you intend to use it often?

But you should never say "Yes, it's more expensive, but it's better" or any other form of acknowledgment that the price is indeed high.

It really is difficult to generalize on the topic of sales, because every business and every price bracket have their specificities, but there's another model that is especially effective when selling rarer or relatively more costly products. It involves having two participants in the process.

Let's have a look at a store selling latex paints of different prices. For the seller, it's more cost effective to sell more expensive paint. They'll make greater profit, and the client will have a top quality paint, with higher durability and better coverage. People don't buy wall paint every day, they only do it when doing repairs at home or elsewhere. They plan their purchases, discuss them with house painters and interior designers. And so a man comes into your store, wishing to buy latex paint, but he heads for the low-end products. If you engage him in conversation and start consulting him, you may manage to convince him to buy a high-end paint – or not. But you'll definitely increase the odds of him spending more money if you apply The Two Salespersons rule, which I will explain in the following paragraphs.

It's not advisable to praise your own merits; that's boasting, and it's quite unappealing. On the other hand, being a qualified expert is an advantage, and people would be more likely to listen to your advice. Guided by this principle, we came up with a sales strategy that we've applied numerous times, and in great many of them it worked like a charm.

If you engage the client in the right way, sooner or later you'll get a question, which you should answer with, "You know, you'd better ask my colleague Ivan; you're in luck that he's here now, because he's the most knowledgeable in this store. So whatever he tells you, listen to him. He's a great expert and will give you the best advice." Whatever the client tries to say at this point, don't let him; just turn around and fetch Ivan.

If you give the client a chance to react, it's highly likely that he stops you from going after Ivan; he may get uncomfortable, having just come to buy a little paint and not feeling special enough to talk to the greatest expert. So don't give him the option to bail out. When Ivan meets the client, the latter will approach him with great respect, because we've built up expectations, we've built an image. And Ivan doesn't even need to be a greater expert than anyone else in the store. He can be any of the other consultants. It's a little manipulative, but very effective – try it, and you'll see for yourself.

When Ivan hears what room needs painting, he'll quickly tell the client what latex he needs. But Ivan also has to act strategically. Ivan is a great expert and very busy, he can't talk a lot and explain in detail. He is polite, but doesn't smile a lot, because he's tired, having so much work and responsibilities. That's what experts are like.

Now let's see what Ivan tells the client. He offers guidance, citing two options: the most expensive paint and an alternative one, still more expensive than the client's choice. Then Ivan excuses himself and goes back to his other duties. In this way, the client cannot react and hesitate in front of Ivan, wondering what to do. He wanted one thing, and now he has two options he doesn't like but can't ignore, because they came from the best expert. The expert is gone, and the client is confused, out of his comfort zone. This is good, because it upsets his logical thinking and disrupts his concentration. The client shouldn't be left alone even for a second, so he's accosted right away by the first player – you. Now you should ask him whether Ivan gave him good advice. If the client is uncertain, he'll probably share that Ivan's suggestions were too expensive. Of course, he may take Ivan's advice and buy the paint, but he'll probably need some time. And it's your job to keep the iron hot, ready for striking. You should tell the man Ivan never disappoints customers, and that people have often come back, regretting that they have ignored his suggestions. Tell the client to think about it, and remind him he's not repainting the house every day, and he'll do the rest himself.

We shouldn't be aggressive, cornering clients and demonstrating our eagerness for them to buy. We only want the best for them, and that's the truth. Every business, in order to be successful and create an effective network of loyal customers, must do what's best for the client.

I'm aware that every business has its unique characteristics, and needs a personalized strategy for communicating with present and potential customers, but I think it won't be a problem for you to adapt what you've learned from this book to the best of your ability.

I have so many strategies under my belt that I can't think of them all now – and it's not even necessary, because they are based on the same principle.

If your business involves presentations before a large audience, or public demonstrations of your products, what comes next is right up your alley.

For a demonstration to be successful, you need not only a group of spectators, but also the right energy and approach to impress your audience. I'll tell you how to achieve this very thing.

Imagine you're making a demonstration of a mandoline slicer, or kitchen knives, or perhaps a new line of nonstick frying pans. The product doesn't matter, the important thing is to make the demonstration fascinating and memorable. Let's say it's a mandoline. First, you take an experienced promoter and train them how to use this multifunctional slicer. They are now quite the experts. It's time to create a strategy so that you gather enough people for your promoter to present before; the group had better be of at least twenty people. But it's possible that the people in your audience feel a bit intimidated by the product's complexity, and fear they won't be able to manage it with ease. That's why we should always have stooges in the audience, also familiar with the product.

And so, the presentation begins, you demonstrate envious cooking speed, marvelous results, and the mandoline is easy to clean and completely safe.

You should be aware of the most common questions that may arise, and have your stooges ask them, because otherwise nobody may dare to, and you won't achieve the desired result.

What people are probably wondering:
– How much does it cost?
– What's the warranty period?
– Will I be able to manage it?
– Can I cut myself?
– Can I damage it?

Perhaps other questions may come up, too. That's why the stooges should play their parts before the presentation ends. While the demonstration is still in progress, people are watching, the presenter allows them to taste some of the delicacies made, and it keeps them engaged. Once the show's over, however, they're likely to disperse quickly.

Let's say Maria is one of our stooges, and Jenny is another. Maria says, "I don't think I can do it", so she's immediately encouraged by the presenter to try. She's hesitant, but at the presenter's insistence, she acquiesces. Maria has no cooking experience, she's holding the mandoline wrong, but it still works wonders, and she's happy.

She ask about the price, and at the same time, Jenny asks another question from the audience: "How long is the warranty period?" The audience gets more involved. The presenter announces the product's regular price, explains the long, 10-year warranty, and finally, the icing on the cake: a super-special offer. It's valid only for the people in the audience, and only for today; tomorrow it would be too late. The product can then be found in the stores at the regular price. Today's a special day, demonstration day; it's natural to have special offers.

Jenny wants to buy the mandoline, and Maria wants one, too. They're excited, radiating happiness. Maria and Jenny are pleased with their purchases, and Jenny wonders aloud whether she should buy one more for a gift. Seeing that, there's a much greater chance that other members of the audience will follow their lead, and much more deals be closed.

FIVE KEY PRINCIPLES
AND MECHANISMS FOR INFLUENCING PEOPLE

There are a few principles that will never let you down and will always come in handy in persuasive communication. I left them for the end of the book because I believe they are extremely important. Some of them were already mentioned in my stories, and I don't want you to forget them. They'll help you find your way to successful sales.

"Find your own path. Those already well-trodden don't lead to treasure!"

–Radoslav Blagoev

THE PRINCIPLE OF CONTRAST

Deals often fall through because the products offered have not been appreciated, and the value exchange does not work to the seller's advantage.

Imagine you are a real estate agent selling a house. You bring your client to a viewing, and they start commenting on minor shortcomings and haggling about the price. However, if you brought them to view another house before the one you've chosen, and that other house was in much worse condition, but asked approximately the same price, you'd activate the Principle of Contrast.

The first house you're showing has damp, moldy walls, a ghastly bathroom and a ton of other problems.

Then you take them to the one you want them to buy. Thus the client will be impressed with the lack of leaks and mold, and notice that the bathroom is not newly furbished, but compared to the previous one is simply wonderful. They'll pay attention to details they wouldn't have noticed if you hadn't triggered the Principle of Contrast.

Now imagine selling a car. It's old, but in decent condition; still, it's second-hand and it shows. Before showing the client your car, show them another of the same model, made the same year, but in much poorer condition. Even if it costs less than yours, you'll still evoke the Principle of Contrast. The client will see the missing trim pieces, the stained seats, the worn out wheel – all things that will deter them from buying. Then, when you show them yours, they'll notice all these elements are in excellent condition, and will appreciate them more than if they had no basis for comparison. The Principle of Contrast will make the buyer pay attention to details they would otherwise ignore. I think you already grasped the idea how important this is. Now you have to adapt it to your strategy, if your business allows it, and you can enjoy easier deals and more satisfied customers.

LOWERING YOUR DEMANDS

This is a unique principle in the area of effective sales and persuasive communication. To help you grasp it right away, let me give you an example.

You have a friend who is always badgering you for money. All of his friends have stopped lending him any, since you are all fed up with his constant requests. You've done responding to him, and never intend to give him a penny because you're certain he won't be paying it pack.

Imagine him coming to you, complaining that he's totally broke and urgently needs a twenty. The chance you'll give it to him is very slim. That's hardly the first time he's asked. If he begged ten people, nine out of them would certainly refuse, as they know him too well. They all know his troubles never end. You're done listening to his excuses, and you know he's in fact just lazy and doesn't bother working. He's a friend of yours, but a slacker all the same.

Now imagine this same friend coming to you, claiming he's in dire need of money. He's in trouble and has to find 3,000 leva as soon as possible. So he comes to you, asking you for a loan of 3000. Of course, the amount is shocking, you're bound to say no, but you're feeling sorry for him, because he seems to be in a real bind this time. When you refuse, he says, "Okay, but can you at least give me 20 or 30 leva so I can go to another friend, I don't have money for tickets even." You feel relieved, it's a dramatically lower demand, so you give him 20 leva – or even 50. You have now managed to save him, parting with a significantly smaller amount.

That's the power of lowering one's demands. You gave him money you would never have spared if he'd asked for it straight away. But now you parted with it easily, without thinking – you wanted to help him out.

Now let me give you another example, straight from business this time. Imagine you import fast-moving consumer goods. For instance, pasta. I don't know why I picked pasta, it may be anything, but let's say you import pasta. You sell it to distributors with 20% trade discount, and each regularly buys around 200 packages a month from you. Now you want to get rid of 500 packages of a brand of pasta that doesn't sell well, so you want it cleared from the storeroom. The question is, how to motivate the distributor to buy it? You know that offering a larger discount may not do the trick. It's just not a popular merchandise, and you have only one shot at this.

So you call the distributor and say, "Hi Ivan, I have some pasta to clear from the storeroom. I'm offering you a great deal; I'll give you 30% discount from the basic price if you can buy 3000 packages. I'm calling you first, because I enjoy our work together, and I don't want you to feel left out."

Ivan refuses out flat, because the quantity is too great and he won't be able to trade it all off. He realizes it's a tempting offer, but it's too much, so he has to say no.

How can you use the lowering demands mechanism? You say, "Okay, wait. I have an idea, I'll call you back in a minute", and then hang up. In thirty minutes, you call again and say, "It's all done, you owe me. I sold 2,500 packages to a distributor at the seaside, and left 500 for you. Now you can have them at the same price, without taking unnecessary risks."

What's the result? Ivan's backed into a corner. First, you now want him to buy only 500 packages of pasta at the same discounted price. Second, you act as if he wanted to buy a smaller quantity from the start. How does that happen? When he refused, he reasoned that it was too large an amount for him to risk. He didn't mention the low demand; the focus was shifted to the number of packages.

Now, if he tries to turn you down with the explanation that the product doesn't sell well, it may sound insulting. Let's see how things may go.

"Look, Martin, it's not a popular product. I'm not sure if I should take even 500 packages."

"Come on, Ivan, what's this about? I thought I was doing you a favor, saving them for you, and now I'll have to find another market for them. But okay, if you don't want them, I'll find somebody who will. Still, think twice about it."

Even if Ivan doesn't buy the pasta, he remains in your debt. With the situation presented like this, he owes you a favor. Tomorrow, when you go to him with another offer, he'll take it. Or when you have a really good deal, don't go to him. Let him find out from elsewhere, and when he inquires why the offer didn't reach him, remind him of the pasta incident. Thus you'll make it clear you thought he was not interested in any bargains, unlike other distributors. There are a few variations, but lowering your demands is a principle I've applied hundreds of times, and it's almost never failed me.

Another example: you'd like to be selling someone's software, but you are willing to do so only if they gave you a 25% trade discount for distributing it; they usually pay no more than 15 to 18% to their partners. Go meet them and ask for a 40% discount. It's a shockingly huge discount, and they'll immediately explain why it cannot be done. Concede and ask for 30%. As a final compromise, ask for 25%; if that is considered too much, it would mean you have no future together. They can hardly refuse you the third time after you lowered your demands so much.

I've achieved discounts that certain companies haven't given anybody else, like 25% from a company who said 12-13% was the absolute maximum. Of course, to get it, I used not only the lowering demands mechanism. I utilized a complete strategy for exerting influence, and achieved excellent results – the same I believe you can get too, if you apply this instrument for successful sales.

THE BOOMERANG PRINCIPLE

This principle involves giving away something without being asked for it, and without expecting anything in return. Just make a gift, and you'll activate this mechanism; it always works and guarantees good results. Even if you don't immediately close a deal, that's a great way to build trust.

Let me illustrate this mechanism so it's easier for you to apply it to your business.

Imagine meeting a potential business partner or a potential client that may order from you regularly. Ask them for an introductory meeting, and don't try selling them anything at that point. Don't sell even if the other side expresses interest. Thus you'll demonstrate that your aim was to get to know each other, not to close a deal immediately. At this meeting, don't give your potential business partner a product from your portfolio, but a nice red pen, saying that red brings luck and you're convinced they'll notice the effect after using it. It must be a luxury pen, but not necessarily branded with your company logo. Explain that the pen brings luck only when gifted to someone. They cannot purchase it or ask someone to buy it for them. They have to receive it by chance, just like in this case. Only then it's lucky. But there's also terms: the receiver should be responsible to the pen, look after it, be careful not to lose it, and always carry it on themselves.

Ask the person before you if they are ready to keep and use this special pen, because if they are going to lose it right away, they'd better not take it at all; it's not a branded product, but a guarantee for future success in various spheres.

With this approach, you're appealing to an integral part of human nature: the tendency to see the world to our advantage. As I already mentioned, people buy lottery tickets, believing they can win, even when the odds are so slim. It's very likely that your potential client uses the red pen a lot. So every time they do so, they'll remember you, and if something nice happens to them, they may associate it with the pen – and you'll become the bringer of luck to that particular client.

When you call them a week later with a specific offer, you'll have a much greater chance for a good deal. And if your offer is a winner, you'll further confirm the client's impression that you're a worthy partner to have.

Let me give you another example.

You're attending a seminar, wishing not only to learn something new from the lecture, but also to meet new people. You choose a seat next to someone who doesn't appear to have come with a large group. Then you go and grab several of the free bottles of water, and upon sitting next to the person, you offer them a bottle, saying you have some extra. By doing so, you've triggered this same mechanism: you've offered a hand, made a gift, although it doesn't cost you a thing, and don't ask for anything in return. Think how often such a thing may have happened to the person next to you. How often have you yourself been given something other than branded goods just like that, without expecting anything? It rarely happens, and all things out of the ordinary are easier to remember. They capture people's attention and open hidden doors in their consciousness, leading to future deals and excellent business relations.

This model often doesn't work so well when corporate identity gets in the way. Remember that. It's not the same whether you give away a nice branded pen – or another branded souvenir – or just a gift. The first is yet another promotional product people don't care for, because they are swamped with these. It's a nice demonstration of goodwill, but it doesn't trigger the boomerang effect. People usually worry that if they don't give a branded gift, in time the person who received it will forget who the gift was from, and the brand won't get impressed on their consciousness. This is not the case. The right present, without a company logo, can leave a much greater impression onto someone's mind. It may be used every day, because it's not promotional merchandise, and then every time the person reaches for it, they'll remember who the gift was from. Or if not ever time, at least regularly.

THE HERD PRINCIPLE

"Whoever doesn't know on which horse to bet, bets on the favorite." That's a perfect illustration of the Herd Principle which you can strategically use in your business.

Most people apply well-known techniques and follow well-known principles, believing that's the only effective way to do sales. While in fact, they never think outside the box, and will never stand out.

Following the Herd Principle, you can tell a customer in your store that a product currently on offer sells like hotcakes, and that's way it's limited in quantity. You are aware that the client may want to buy lots of it, but unfortunately, you can only sell them five packages at a time. What happens when an offer is phrased like that? You trigger more than one persuasive mechanism.

First, you activate the Herd Principle – it's such a great bargain that everyone buys it. It's natural for the client to go with the flow and strive to be like everyone else. Second, even before knowing the client's opinion on your offer, you are setting terms, which shifts the focus from "Should I buy it?" to "How can I buy more?". How does that happen? People see the world to their advantage and are selfish by nature, and when something is limited, but mass produced, we wish to take more than the others. I know this statement will offend Yellows, who rarely try to take advantage and would probably never like a book such as this, and even condone such strategies. But truth is, an expert knowledge of the mechanisms of persuasive communication can be employed for the promotion of good causes just as easily as for selling goods and services.

Now, reading about the Herd Principle, you can probably recall the example I gave you of the product demonstration, and the stooges wishing to buy it and commenting how good it was. You remember it, don't you? It was a good illustration of the Herd Principle.

SCARCITY PRINCIPLE

Imagine you work in a home appliances store, and you see people looking at the washing machines. You watch them and notice they come back to consider a particular model twice. It seems to have impressed them with either its price or its features, it doesn't matter. At this point, they are still hesitant, and there's a 30% chance that they won't buy the product, exactly due to uncertainty.

In such a situation, most sellers would volunteer information only if approached by the customer. They would list the product's technical features, or, as I'd like to put it, would consult the client on the machine's many advantages. Instead, they could trigger the scarcity mechanism. Here's a sample conversation.

"Hello, I see you're looking at this wonderful washing machine, but unfortunately, we just sold the last one available. This one is saved for a client who ordered it online. Do you want me to show you other great models?"

In such a situation, you can be sure that the very product you claimed was unavailable, will suddenly become the most desirable one. Demand and scarcity provoke a stronger interest in buyers and help them make up their mind that they need this very product and nothing else.

A possible scenario:

"What a pity! We've just decided to buy this very washing machine, but I guess we'll have to look for it elsewhere."

"No, no, we don't like disappointing our customers. If you're really sure this is your final choice, I'll see what I can do. Give me five minutes."

In five minutes, you return with good news (as I already mentioned, it's great to be the bringer of good news.)

"It's alright, I arranged everything. We'll give you the washing machine we set aside for the online order, and then send our client one from another of our stores. What do you say?"

In this way, you not only strike a good deal, but manage to make people happy. Everyone wants to get lucky, to believe in their good fortune. You will not only sell a product and please your client, but receive special thanks for your cooperation.

Now you are aware of the power of scarcity, and I believe you can successfully apply this mechanism in your business. With this last example, I want to impress upon you another crucial thing for your success. Whatever you see in your mind, that's what you have in your life.

I have business people telling me on a daily basis that there's no market in Bulgaria, it's too limited a market, people here cannot afford much, business here can't flourish, and tons of similar nonsense. Remember, if you've decided to buy a particular car, right after making up your mind, you'll start noticing more and more of this very model on the road.

If you believe there's no market, for you there will be none. If you think there is no business, for you there will be none. If you are convinced the product you offer is very hard to sell, you're guaranteed to have difficulties. If you are afraid you can't make money out of what you're doing, you won't be making any.

Thank you for reading my book. I believe what you learned from it will be useful, will improve your business and have a positive effect on your personal development.

CONCLUSION

That's the last point I want to make, but it's just as important as the things I already shared.

It's not necessary to constantly come up with new offers and bargains to attract consumers' attention. In most cases, emotional engagement bonuses remain unannounced and hidden.

The effect is much stronger when you offer the bonus immediately after purchase. In this case, the last thing to happen to the client in the store is getting a gift. Their visit to your store ends on a positive note, with a gift and a smile. A bit like the dessert after a meal.

You can announce giving away free dessert to anyone who makes a purchase, or simply give them free desert without announcing it first. It makes a whole lot of difference. Unannounced bonuses lead to emotional engagement, and then the story about you and your great behavior spreads like wildfire. People love sharing things that don't happen to them every day.

When was the last time you received a bonus after making a purchase? An unannounced bonus with no strings attached? Such things rarely happen, and thus are much more effective in the long run, which should be your goal.

Focus on relationship potential instead on one-time deals, unless the deal is your last before you retire.

Each marketing activity has to serve a particular purpose and be traceable. We should know the result of our efforts and experiments, otherwise we won't be improving at all.

At a digital marketing seminar, the lector discussed all the possibilities Facebook can offer, and asked people, "Have you tried promoting your content in this way? What about that way?" "Did you know you can do this? What about that?" He listed all the functions and types of promotional activities of this medium, but marketing is much more than posting and knowing the technical side of things. It's a state of mind. To be successful, you need to think strategically and analyze.

For a client of ours, we did a series of digital campaigns and compared results. Finally, we realized consumers didn't buy as much as we wanted because they found it too time-consuming to read and watch videos to understand how to use the product. Our analyses showed that feedback was extremely important, and that was the real issue. On the client's website there was a contact form and a phone number, but people rarely used it. They browsed the site, scanned through the content, and most of them left without making an order. Many visitors spent as long as thirty minutes on the website, but still didn't buy. There was a problem, and we suspected people were worried whether they would be able to handle the product, whether it would be too difficult to use, etc.

Then we came up with the idea of a promotional video with a phone number integrated in the image. We posted it, but nothing happened; everything continued as before. So we took the number out of the image and added it in the social media post itself. Now the results were instantaneous. Orders through the webpage dwindled, almost stopped. But the phone kept ringing. Why was that happening now, when the number had always been there on the website? And why nothing changed when the number was perfectly visible as part of the image, while now it was in the post itself, so many people called it?

When the number is part of the image, it can't be dialed directly if you come across the ad on a mobile device. To call it, you must memorize it first and then dial it, which is an impediment in communication, and our results marked it as an ineffective solution. However, when the number is written in the post itself, it can be dialed straight away, no need of memorizing. It may look like an insignificant detail, but proved of utmost importance.

That's why you shouldn't underestimate subtle changes in your communication. You should constantly analyze and optimize your communication strategies, so that you can offer ever more elaborate and effective business solutions.

I hope you found this book useful and intriguing. I invested lots of my scarce free time in writing it. I could have given many more examples, but I don't think the book needs any stuffing. I aimed at providing valuable and concise information on effective sales and successful communication. Now it is all in your hands – just as it always was. I believe you can apply what you've learned to your business and communication strategies.

Thank you for your time. And don't forget: to advertise and sell is an art.

"There's room for everyone at the top. The important thing is, when you get there, not to be too tired to enjoy the view."

—Radoslav Blagoev

BUSINESS ABOVE THE RED LINE

Fulfil your business potential or start a successful business from scratch

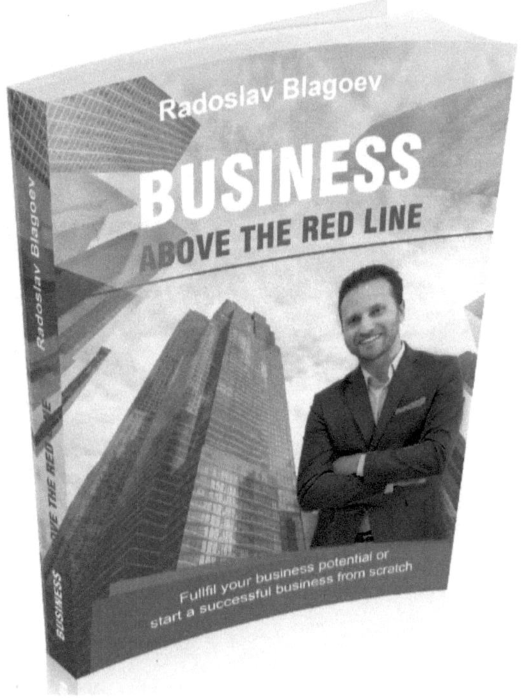

Business above the Red Line is based on Radoslav Blagoev's broad practical experience. Having consulted hundreds of companies and even more entrepreneurs, he provides valuable advice and offers well-summarized information that will help you create a strong business model and marketing strategy, which will in turn make you stand out among your rivals and increase your competitiveness.

*I recognized many of my own mistakes in **Business above the Red Line**. An extremely useful book, presenting the information in a very concise fashion. I strongly recommend it to any entrepreneur.*

–Maria Stoyanova

This book has to be taught at school. Very useful, I read it twice and I've underlined it all. I didn't expect a Bulgarian to publish a book on par with foreign authors.

–Ivan Vladimirov

*This book is as good as **Read the Signs**; yet another great book by Radoslav. I'm looking forward to his future works as well.*

–Nikolina Georgieva

***Business above the Red Line** turned over a new leaf for my business. I didn't expect much, but I'm really impressed by how useful this book turned out. I'm glad we have Bulgarian authors who are so knowledgeable and willing to share their expertise.*

–Marietta Topalova

*Once more, I'm inspired and full of new ideas. I've reread **Read the Signs** several times, and now I keep **Business above the Red Line** on my nightstand, because it couldn't be read only once. I wish the author good health, and I hope his books reach more businesspeople, because they are extremely helpful.*

–Maria Bachvarova

*I've read lots of business-oriented books, but **Read the Signs** is definitely the best book on sales. I was greatly impressed that **Business above the Red Line** was just as captivating and useful. I now follow Radoslav closely because he has much to share about business running, and he's such an inspiration. I wish him health and success.*

–Martin Ahchiev

YOU LEAD

YOU LEAD is a must-read for every entrepreneur. Using numerous examples, the author demonstrates that success and results are the projection of different business owners and managers' thinking. He also lists the most common problems, mistakes, and oversights in their business activities and behavior. YOU LEAD has a strong emotional impact and manages to inspire entrepreneurs. It helps shift their perspective, which leads to a quick change in their business results.

THE FIRST
MAGNETIC STRATEGIC
BUSINESS GAME IN
THE WORLD

You have an entrepreneurial spirit – otherwise, you wouldn't be reading this book. That's why, I'd like to very briefly introduce you to a unique board game, YOU LEAD.

It took me and my team more than three years to design the game and finally be happy with the results. It has gone a long way of improvement and optimization until we reached a variation that evoked a vast complexity of emotions in the players.

The game allows for participants to employ different strategies every time, which makes it unique because no two plays can be identical. You decide whether to start a business franchise or perhaps a service business.

Your employees' training or the number of people you hire is also up to you, but not only because you are well aware that competent experts are rare and not readily available.

The game is characterized by dynamic gameplay due to its large number of elements and dynamic sectors, which affect you in different ways depending on your business strategy. And last but not least, it is an extremely fun game that will improve your business thinking, marketing skills, and entrepreneurial intuition.

Welcome to the red business ocean where each company starts and grows its business in a highly competitive environment. Surviving isn't easy, and taking the lead and gaining market share can be a real challenge. Improve your business skills while playing. Make mistakes in the game so you can avoid them in real life. Develop your business intuition because it will come in handy. The competition will always be breathing down your neck, so be on your guard and don't forget: YOU LEAD!

www.ingramcontent.com/pod-product-compliance
Lightning Source LLC
LaVergne TN
LVHW091701190726
843493LV00001B/89